Saving Civilization

Jeb Taylor

Unless otherwise noted, word definitions
are taken from Merriam-Webster: Webster's Third
New International Dictionary, Unabridged
(Merriam-Webster, 2002, http://unabridged.merriam-webster.com).

All information relating to the Tanakh is taken from Tanakh:
The Holy Scriptures *copyright © 1985 by The*
Jewish Publication Society.

All information relating to the Old and New Testaments of
the Holy Bible is taken from the King James Version of the Holy Bible.

Portions of this work were previously published under the same title by Cold
River Studio.

ISBN10: 1479324132
ISBN13: 9781479324132

Saving Civilization is dedicated to future generations,
whose quality of life depends on the wisdom
of the decisions that we make today.

Contents

6

Figures

Preface

Somewhere in the Middle East, around 12,000 thousand years ago, a small group of migratory foragers made a decision that profoundly influenced the course of humankind. They decided to adopt agriculture as their primary subsistence strategy.

That decision was almost certainly made in an attempt to provide them with increased survival security, which it certainly did—at least over the short-term. But it also inadvertently set humankind on a course of artificial development that has severely, adversely affected other members of our species, other species, and the environment: conditions that threaten, rather than enhance, our long-term survival prospects.

We may be able to continue on as we have for a few more decades, or even generations, but the present manifestation of artificial development is too destructive to be maintained, if it is not altered, civilization will collapse in the not too distant future. This leads to two pertinent questions:

- Can civilization be saved?
- Should civilization be saved?

An early draft of *Saving Civilization* was sent to a number of respected individuals for their comments. Among them was Farley Mowat, one of Canada's most renowned and respected naturalists. As regards the second question, he responded:

> I am by no means convinced that saving civilization is a good idea. In fact, you are so persuasive in your description of what

is wrong with it that you are confirming my belief that it's time that we got rid of this particular human disease.

Farley Mowat has devoted much of his life to raising public awareness regarding the destructive nature of civilization, so his response was both unexpected and sobering. Consequently, a revised draft was sent to him hoping that it would elicit a more positive reaction. It did not. He responded:

> I'm even more convinced than ever that Homo sapiens is a lost cause. And that the sooner we become extinct, the better the prospects are for the ongoing survival and evolution of animate creation.

Farley's perspectives may seem unduly negative, but they are actually quite valid. The present manifestation of civilization is so destructive to other species and the environment that, arguably, no effort should be made to preserve or save it.

But there are aspects of human behavior that suggest we are capable of attaining a higher state of civilization, one that is sustainable and not unduly destructive. Cultivating that aspect of human behavior is the goal of *Saving Civilization.*

Achieving a sustainable state of existence is possible, but it will require that we profoundly modify our behavior—which will require that we achieve much higher levels of awareness than we currently have—which will require that we examine ourselves, our motives, our beliefs, and our accomplishments with a degree of candor that we are generally wont to do.

In this discussion, readers will encounter a number of unorthodox viewpoints and perspectives. When they do, they are asked to consider that orthodoxy is not working for us and that carefully vetted alternatives should be considered. All of the viewpoints and perspectives offered in this discussion are objective, intended to raise awareness, and to encourage proactivity in the pursuit of sustainability.

~ ~ ~ ~

Please note:

- *Specific definitions for keywords, initially listed in bold type, are provided in the Glossary.*

- *It is highly recommended that readers begin at the preface and continue sequentially through to the last chapter. Information, concepts, and explanations are provided along the way that are needed to fully comprehend what follows.*

Part I – Becoming Human

Man has lost the capacity to foresee and forestall.
We will end by destroying the earth.

—Albert Schweitzer

1: In the Beginning…

I have found the missing link between the higher apes and civilized man: it is us.

—*Konrad Lorenz*

Anthropological evidence suggests that Homo sapiens evolved out of an earlier Homo line somewhere in east-central Africa about 175,000 years ago. While 175,000 years may seem like a long period of time, from an evolutionary perspective, it is not. We are actually members of one of the most recent species to appear on Earth.

Very little is known about our earliest ancestors. If they behaved similarly to members of more recent foraging societies, however, they probably practiced various, mostly sustainable, foraging subsistence strategies, lived in small **egalitarian** extended family groups, and migrated seasonally throughout their ranges to utilize available resources.

2: Becoming Human

One never knows how loyalty is born.

—Robert Morse

We share many traits and characteristics with our Homo ancestors, but we possess other traits that make us uniquely human. Notably, we are: more sociable, more adaptable, better able to conceptualize, and we are capable of conveying information and concepts abstractly through various forms of communication.

SOCIABILITY

Initially individuals of all species were probably completely egocentric. They were primarily concerned with *their* own survival and reproduction. When and why species began to assume sociable behavior is unknown. It is likely, though, that the first species to do so were insects, and that the earliest social behavior consisted of females caring for *their* eggs or males guarding *their* females.

Since then, the level of sociability assumed by some species has advanced significantly. But most members of most of species are still completely egocentric. This suggests that sociability is not necessarily an essential survival mechanism for individuals or species.

Why members of some species exhibit a willingness to sacrifice some of their personal survival prospects to enhance the survival prospects of others is a mystery. It is not too difficult to understand why females might be motivated to protect their eggs, but why would males assume the risk of protecting females? *Current Biology* offers a plausible explanation by citing a study of wild, individually marked and genotyped field crickets:

> Lone females or males suffer similar rates of predation, but when a pair is attacked, the male allows the female priority access to their burrow and in doing so dramatically increases his probability of being killed. In compensation for this increased predation risk, paired males mate more frequently and father more of the female's offspring. By staying with a male, females increase the sperm contribution of preferred males as well as reducing their predation risk.[1]

There are obviously fundamental differences between insects guarding eggs or mates and the establishment of complex societies by humans, but the progression between them is clear. Selflessness opens the door to interdependency, and interdependency leads inevitably to cooperation—all of which are fundamental to the establishment of complex human societies.

In the context of this discussion, sociability will be regarded as a willingness of individuals to accept increased risk to their own survival to enhance the survival prospects of other members of their species.

Within the animal kingdom, social insects establish the most efficient societies, because their members are extremely selfless, completely interdependent, and willing to cooperate with each other. But insect sociability is strictly familial.

Social ant, termite, and bee societies, for example, consist of single breeding females who are fertilized by single males. The queens then produce infertile female daughters who do not have to compete with each

---

1 http://www.cell.com/current-biology/abstract/S0960-9822(11)00959-6?switch=standard

other to survive or procreate. Their responsibilities are devoted solely to supporting and protecting their societies. In that way they contribute *indirectly* to the perpetuation of their own genetic lineage. Their existence may seem unfulfilling to us, but from an evolutionary perspective, their survival strategy has proven extremely successful.

Conversely, modern human societies are far more complex, but nowhere near as efficient. Our societies are composed of unrelated, fertile males and females who must compete with other members of their societies to survive and procreate—hardly conditions that encourage social solidarity.

Nevertheless, humans are the most compassionate creatures on Earth. This enables us to not only cooperate with individuals we are not related to—and have to compete with, it frequently compels us to act selflessly in their behalf. Sociability is what enables us to coexist in large complex societies, and if fostered, it may eventually enable us to achieve comprehensive inter-societal solidarity, a condition essential in the attainment of sustainable existence.

But our commitments to sociability are easily sidetracked by other commitments, desires, and needs, all of which are becoming more pressing as our societies grow increasingly larger and more complex.

ADAPTABILITY

For the first hundred thousand years of human existence, our ancestors remained in central Africa and advanced very little. Then, about seventy-five thousand years ago, deteriorating climatic conditions forced them to move southward and northward into temperate zones (those south of latitudes 23.5 degrees south and north of latitude 23.5 degrees north). At that time, they began to exhibit one of their most remarkable survival traits: adaptability. Moving into temperate zones forced them to modify their subsistence strategies from foraging to foraging *and* hoarding.

Hoarding is an essential survival strategy for many species living in temperate areas. Temperate zones exist because Earth revolves around the sun annually on a tilted axis. For half of each year, the northern hemisphere is tilted toward the sun and experiences an active growing season (summer), while the southern hemisphere is tilted away from it and experiences an inactive (or dormant) season (winter). Conversely, during the other half of the year, the southern hemisphere is tilted toward the sun, while the northern hemisphere is tilted away from it, reversing the seasons.

Seasonal inactivity refers specifically to terrestrial plants, but since most animal species, including our own, rely directly or indirectly on plants for their own sustenance, winters in temperate zones present significant survival challenges for them.

Terrestrial animal species employ various survival strategies to cope with winters. Species capable of long-distance flight, such as some birds and insects, migrate north and south to avoid winters. Many that do not—such as most reptile, amphibian, insect, and some mammal species—resort to hibernation. Animals that do not migrate or hibernate, such as our own species, are forced to hoard food when it is available and store it in caches and/or as body fat for future use.

Hoarding is an often overlooked, but important, survival strategy to consider when trying to unravel the intricacies of human behavior. Our ability to successfully incorporate it into our subsistence strategy has enabled us to thrive in temperate climates. Unfortunately, hoarding has evolved into a compulsion responsible for many of the problems that now threaten civilization, ranging from inter-societal polarity and conflict, to loss of biota and environmental degradation.

In any event, within less than sixty-five thousand years after moving into temperate zones, our specie's ability to adapt to different environmental conditions enabled us to find and settle almost every habitable area on every continent on Earth. That type of species expansion, especially for pedestrian creatures, is unprecedented. Clearly, there is something very different about us.

CONCEPTUALIZATION

Humans, unlike other species, have the capacity to conceptualize. Conceptualization is the key that opened the door to increased awareness and rampant **artificial** development. But it is important to realize that the conceptualization process is flawed. Even when utilizing the most credible information available, it can—and frequently does—lead to the formation of misconceptions rather than increased awareness. A classic example of this condition is the longstanding misconception regarding the motions of celestial bodies.

Geocentrism was an astronomical model proposed by the Greek philosopher Anaximander in the sixth century BCE.[2] It maintained that Earth was at the center of the universe, and that the Sun, Moon, stars, and other celestial bodies revolved around it. That conclusion was based on the observation that most heavenly bodies *appeared* to rise above Earth's eastern horizon, travel across the sky, and set below Earth's western horizon.

Most learned people believed that the geocentric model had merit, but a consensus regarding it was never reached because it could not explain the motions and locations of *all* of the celestial bodies, *all* of the time.

It wasn't until the sixteenth century that Nicholaus Copernicus conceptualized that although the Moon did revolve around Earth, that Earth rotated on an axis, and that it and the other planets revolved around the sun. That insight became known as the heliocentric model, and once it was proposed, a consensus was quickly reached regarding it because it did account for the motions and locations of *all* of the celestial bodies, *all* of the time.

The fact that the geocentric model misconception was perpetuated for two thousand years is graphic evidence that our ability to conceptualize is subject to error, but the fact that the model was eventually discarded in favor of the heliocentric model is evidence that the process, even if belatedly, does work. *The important consideration regarding conceptualization is that concepts be amendable as more information becomes available.*

---

2 http://en.wikipedia.org/wiki/Geocentric_model

COMMUNICATION

The ability to conceptualize enabled us to be creative, but it was our ability to convey concepts, opinions, beliefs, and information abstractly through various forms of communication that enabled us to become the dominant mammal species on Earth.

Human behavior, like that of all species, is determined by various combinations of instinctive and learned behavior. Unlike other species, however, our behavior is dominated by what we learn *abstractly* from each other.

The ability to convey information abstractly is a fundamental aspect of civilized existence. In this discussion, information will be divided into three primary and one secondary category:

- accurate information

  o misinformation

- disinformation, and

- **dogma**

The reliability of information depends, to a large degree, on the motive for its dissemination. Unfortunately, there are no words in the English language that specifically recognize different motives for disseminating information. Consequently, in this discussion, the terms *education, deception,* and *indoctrination* will be used with the following specific definitions:

- **education**: the conveyance of accurate information intended to foster greater awareness (Author)

  o miseducation: the unintentional conveyance of misinformation (Author)

- **deception**: the conveyance of disinformation intended to persuade through deceit (Author)

- **indoctrination**: the conveyance of dogma intended to persuade through **faith** (Author)

Our success utilizing abstract learning is a wonder, because we are incredibly indiscriminate in its use. We are just as likely, for example, to assimilate misinformation, disinformation, or dogma as we are accurate information.

Our susceptibility to the dissemination of unreliable information is a chronic problem intrinsic to the abstract learning process. Obviously, we cannot be expected to behave rationally or responsibly if we are always handicapped with misconceptions, deceptions, and delusions. Fortunately, we have the capacity to *learn how to learn better* (see Chapter 13: Increase Awareness).

EDUCATION

Although the purpose of education is to increase awareness through the dissemination of accurate information, it also unintentionally disseminates misinformation, which, unfortunately, inevitably leads to the formation of misconceptions. Consequently, education must always be regarded as a dynamic process open to revision as additional information becomes available. Only in that way can education be counted on to impart knowledge and increase awareness. A case in point was the long-standing misconception regarding the motions of celestial bodies just described.

DECEPTION

Deception is frequently presented as education, but it is not. Its intention is to persuade through the intentional dissemination of misinformation. Deceptions are usually conveyed to directly or indirectly advance the positions of those who *initially* conceived them.

Unfortunately, our capacity to assimilate information abstractly makes us extremely susceptible to the dissemination of disinformation through deception. Unfortunately, self-serving individuals in government, business, and religion shamelessly exploit this susceptibility.

Hermann Göring, a prominent leader in the Nazi party and commander of the German Luftwaffe during World War II, explained the process of deception to Gustave Gilbert, an American psychologist, who interviewed him at the Nuremburg war trials in 1947:[3]

> Göring: Why, of course, the people don't want war. Why should some poor slob on a farm want to risk his life in a war when the best that he can get out of it is to come back to his farm in one piece. Naturally, the common people don't want war, neither in Russia nor in England nor in America, nor for that matter in Germany. That is understood. But after all, it is the leaders of the country who determine the policy and it is always a simple matter to drag the people along, whether it is a democracy or a fascist dictatorship or a Parliament or a Communist dictatorship.
>
> Gilbert: There is one difference. In a democracy, the people have some say in the matter through their elected representatives, and in the United States only Congress can declare wars.
>
> Göring: Oh, that is all well and good, but, voice or no voice, the people can always be brought to the bidding of the leaders. That is easy. All you have to do is tell them they are being attacked and denounce the pacifists for lack of patriotism and exposing the country to danger. It works the same way in any country.[4]

Most of us would like to believe that citizens of modern, progressive societies like the United States would not be susceptible to that type of deception, but we are, as recent events have proven.

---

3 http://en.wikipedia.org/wiki/Gustave_Gilbert
4 http://en.wikiquote.org/wiki/Hermann_G%C3%B6ring

Soon after the al-Qaeda attacks on the World Trade Center and Pentagon in 2001, for example, former president George W. Bush began a deception campaign to garner support for an invasion of Iraq. Listed below are a number of excerpts from his 2002 and 2003 speeches that support this claim:

Cincinnati, October 7, 2002

Right now, Iraq is expanding and improving facilities that were used for the production of biological weapons.

We know that the regime has produced thousands of tons of chemical agents, including mustard gas, sarin nerve gas, [and] VX nerve gas.

The evidence indicates that Iraq is reconstituting its nuclear weapons program. Saddam Hussein has held numerous meetings with Iraqi nuclear scientists, a group he calls his "nuclear Mujahideen"—his nuclear holy warriors. Satellite photographs reveal that Iraq is rebuilding facilities at sites that have been part of its nuclear program in the past. Iraq has attempted to purchase high-strength aluminum tubes and other equipment needed for gas centrifuges, which are used to enrich uranium for nuclear weapons.

Intelligence gathered by this and other governments leaves no doubt that the Iraqi regime continues to possess and conceal some of the most lethal weapons ever devised.

The Iraqi regime possesses and produces chemical and biological weapons. It is seeking nuclear weapons…. If we know Saddam Hussein has dangerous weapons today—and we do—does it make any sense for the world to wait to confront him as he grows even stronger and develops even more dangerous weapons?

We know that the regime has produced thousands of tons of chemical agents, including mustard gas, sarin nerve gas, [and] VX nerve gas.

We've also discovered through intelligence that Iraq has a growing fleet of manned and unmanned aerial vehicles that could be used to disperse chemical or biological weapons across broad areas. We're concerned that Iraq is exploring ways of using these UAVs for missions targeting the United States.

State of the Union Address, January 28, 2003

Our intelligence officials estimate that Saddam Hussein had the materials to produce as much as 500 tons of sarin, mustard, and VX nerve agent.

The British government has learned that Saddam Hussein recently sought significant quantities of uranium from Africa. Our intelligence sources tell us that he has attempted to purchase high-strength aluminum tubes suitable for nuclear weapons production. Saddam Hussein has not credibly explained these activities. He clearly has much to hide.

Evidence from intelligence sources, secret communications, and statements by people now in custody reveal that Saddam Hussein aids and protects terrorists, including members of al-Qaeda.

Address to the Nation, March 17, 2003

Intelligence gathered by this and other governments leaves no doubt that the Iraqi regime continues to possess and conceal some of the most lethal weapons ever devised. This regime has already used weapons of mass destruction against Iraq's neighbors and against Iraq's people.[5]

---

5 http://www.roadtopeace.org/research.php?itemid=319

Bush's deceptions convinced most Americans that we had no choice but to invade Iraq. As it turned out, though, *none* of his allegations were true. Consequently, the American public was deceived into supporting the invasion of a sovereign nation that posed no immediate threat to us, or our allies that was eventually responsible for:[6]

- 4,385 US troop deaths,

- between one hundred thousand and 1.2 million Iraqi deaths (mostly civilian),[7]

- 31,716 US troop injuries (official); over one hundred thousand (estimated),

- an unknown number of Iraqi troop and civilian injuries,

- over one million Iraqi civilians displaced from their homes,

- a financial cost to the United States of about $714 billion,[8]

- the justifiable loss of a great deal of international respect, and

- a dramatic increase in international political and religious tension and polarization

This is just one of many thousands of examples that could be cited to illustrate the damage that can occur when individuals or organizations employ deception to elicit support for themselves or their policies.

INDOCTRINATION

The motive behind indoctrination is far more complex than deception and can be far more insidious, because it leads to *fixed* misconceptions and

6 http://www.antiwar.com/casualties/
7 http://www.antiwar.com/casualties/
8 http://costofwar.com/

delusions that can be almost impossible to amend. Indoctrination is generally used to disseminate dogma intended to advance specific religious, political, economic, social, or other ideologies—the assimilation of which may or may not advance the positions of those who promote them.

Some degree of indoctrination may be necessary to establish and maintain solidarity within social groups, but without ever having tried to establish or maintain solidarity without it, we really don't know. We do know that one of the most expedient ways to establish solidarity is through indoctrination, and that we are very susceptible to it. We also know that self-serving individuals regularly exploit our susceptibility. In fact, most of our religious, political, economic, social, and other ideological beliefs are nothing more than dogmas we have been indoctrinated with.

Dogmas are not necessarily *false* beliefs, but the most pervasive of them are those that cannot be proved or disproved, which makes them, at least, *irrational* beliefs. Additionally, because they cannot be disproved, they are ideal mediums for charlatans to use to advance their own positions and ideologies.

Remarkably, dogmas, no matter how improbable they may be, can be successfully disseminated. A case in point is the near global acceptance of Abrahamic religious dogmas. They are extremely improbable, but they have been so well promoted that more than half of the people on Earth now believe in them. (See chapter 7: Religion).

In an attempt to deal with biblical improbability issues, Abrahamic religious clerics claim that their dogmas are derived from scriptures that were given to them by God and cannot, therefore, be judged by the same standards as everything else (God works in mysterious ways). Additionally, their scriptures make it clear that to question or challenge them is tantamount to questioning or challenging God, and that doing so will incur his wrath.

Nevertheless, religious doctrines are generally so improbable that very few adults would take them seriously if first exposed to them as adults. Religious indoctrination, therefore, must begin with young children who are less suspicious and more trusting. Once they have been successfully

indoctrinated with a religion's dogmas, they will generally remain support-
ive of that religion for the remainder of their lives.

Perversely, indoctrination typically includes provisions that encourage—or require—parents to subject their own children to the same
indoctrination processes they were subjected to when they were children,
thus ensuring its perpetuation.

The successful promotion of dogma may help to maintain solidarity
within social groups and support for them, but it inevitably incites polarity
between them that leads to conflict and violence. So much polarity exists
between members of the various Abrahamic religions, for example, that
even though they all believe in the same god and recognize most of the
same prophets, they have been killing each other continuously for more
than thirteen centuries.

RELIABILITY OF SOURCES

PARENTS

It would be nearly impossible to overstate how much influence parents have
on their children's awareness and behavior. Parents are, in a very real sense,
role models for their children. Regardless of the quality of parent–child
relationships, children will generally respond to issues in much the same
way their parents do. If parents maintain irrational ideological political,
religious, economic, racial, sexist, homophobic, or other beliefs, so, generally, will their children—as will their children, and on and on in perpetuity.

In natural states of existence, parental instruction is an ideal way to provide offspring with the knowledge and skills they need to survive as adults.
In our current artificial state of existence, however, individuals assimilate
so much misinformation, disinformation, and dogma throughout their
lives—that they cannot be regarded as reliable role models or sources of
information for their children.

This problem isn't necessarily intrinsic to artificial development, it is cultural. If individuals were not subjected to so much misinformation, disinformation, and dogma throughout their lives—and were encouraged/allowed to be more aware, they would logically prove to be more reliable role models and sources of information for their children.

SCHOOL

Schools also have an enormous impact on our awareness and behavior. Teachers are generally regarded as educators, but their primary responsibilities are actually to prepare children to be good citizens. Good citizens in this context can be defined as individuals who are loyal to their societies, productive within their societies, and obedient to their leaders.

Theoretically, those goals could be achieved solely through education if societies maintained very high standards of behavior. Because most societies have relied upon aggressive, competitive developmental strategies to establish themselves, however, few of them do. Consequently, most societies rely on deceptive curricula to "enhance" their respectability.

A case in point is the American grade school version of the "discovery" and initial "settlement" of the New World by Christopher Columbus[9].

In elementary school, children are taught that Columbus discovered America in 1492. That claim is a deception. The New World was actually discovered and settled twelve thousand years earlier by intrepid explorers from central Asia. Columbus wasn't even the first European to reach America. That distinction goes to the Norse who established a settlement in Newfoundland, Canada five hundred years earlier. Columbus's primary distinction is that he was the first *Christian* to establish a settlement in the New World.

Students are taught that Native Americans inhabited the New World when Columbus arrived, but that their cultures were primitive and therefore relatively inconsequential. That is another deception. Many hundreds

---

9 Since writing this, I corresponded with a respected grade school teacher who assured me that curricula are far more objective today than when I attended grade school.

of firmly established nations existed in the New World at that time. In fact, the Incan empire centered out of Cajamarca in Peru, the Mayan empire centered out of Tikal in Guatemala, and the Aztec empire centered out of Tenochtitlan in Mexico were all larger and arguably more culturally advanced than any societies in Europe at that time.

Historical deceptions are perpetuated not only through the dissemination of disinformation but through the omission of pertinent information. Students are not, for example, generally taught that when Columbus settled Hispaniola (present-day Haiti and the Dominican Republic), that the entire indigenous Taino population there was enslaved and forced to work for them. Enslavement was apparently a foremost thought on Columbus's mind at that time. The following was excerpted from his diary on the day he landed in Hispaniola: Sunday, December 16, 1492:

> They have no weapons or fighting skills…. They are very timid: three men could put a thousand of them to flight, so they could easily be commanded and made to work, to sow, and do whatever might be needed…. (Cummins 1992, 142)

No one knows exactly what the pre-Columbian Taino population of Hispaniola was. Estimates vary enormously, but it is generally believed to have been at least three to four hundred thousand. In any event, due primarily to the oppressive conditions established there by Columbus, within just over sixty years, *all* of the Taino had been worked to death in mines, sold away as slaves, died from disease, killed for dog food, or chosen suicide as preferable to living under the oppressive conditions imposed by the Spanish (Loewen 1995, 55).

Columbus was arguably a thoroughly contemptible human being. Because we are unwilling to face the dark side of our history, however, we are forced to perpetuate the deception that he was an admirable man. And in an attempt to validate that deception, we even honor him with a national holiday.

If this was an isolated incident, it would still be alarming, but it is not. Euro-Americans vanquished hundreds of indigenous nations so they could establish their own settlements in North and South America. Additionally, for nearly 350 years, they relied heavily on oppressive slave labor to build them.

Today, we are incredibly sensitive to injustices perpetrated by other nations, but because we continue to deceive ourselves about ourselves, we remain oblivious to the injustices we perpetrated toward others: most notably, Native Americans (whose land we stole) and African Americans (whose forced labor we relied on to build this country).

There are many aspects of American history that are actually quite shameful. Consequently, societies/schools must rely on deception to help cultivate pride and patriotism in students.

The primary purpose of "education" in grades 1-12 is to prepare *most* students to support and defend their societies. The secondary purpose is to identify and prepare *some* students to go on to university levels of "education."

At the university level, deceptions begin to coincide and merge with ideological perspectives and policies. Medical, engineering, biotech, agricultural, financial, and other special interests attempt to influence curricula that favors their policies, practices, and ideologies by establishing "partnerships" through "contributions."

Steve Halverson, CEO of the Haskell Company and chair of the Florida Council 100, claims that "partnerships" between colleges and businesses make sense. He maintains:

> Businesses are consumers of the products of higher education. [Higher education institutions] produce talent in intellectual capital that is consumed in business and put to productive use in society.[10]

This may be true, but allowing businesses to establish partnerships with universities is arguably not wise. It is, after all, graduates from universities that societies rely on to establish responsible behavioral paradigms in the future. This is something they will find very difficult to do if they have

---

10 http://diverseeducation.com/article/50016/

been subjected to curriculums influenced by corporations who are motivated primarily by personal profit, rather than concern for the welfare of individuals, societies, civilization, other species, or the environment.

Schools have an incredible opportunity to increase public awareness at all grade levels. Unfortunately, they are not currently utilizing their potential very well at all.

CHURCH

It is difficult to assess just how much impact churches actually have on human awareness and behavior, but it is enormous. This impact is nearly universally regarded as positive, but clerics in churches disseminate religious dogma to establish devotion through persuasion, *not* to increase awareness. Consequently, that assumption needs to be challenged. This will be done as we proceed. For now, it is only pertinent to note that churches are not reliable, or even credible, sources of information.

THE MEDIA

Currently, most of us rely on various media agencies to supply us with current, pertinent news and information. Unfortunately, very few media agencies are free to report objectively. They can be influenced by governmental regulations and are owned and controlled by corporations with very biased self-serving perspectives.

GOVERNMENT INTERVENTION

The First Amendment to the US Constitution ensures the right to free speech, but that right has been suppressed a number of times by political administrations seeking to inhibit opposition to themselves or their policies since its inception in 1791. The most noteworthy examples are:

- The Alien and Sedition Act of 1798, initiated by John Adams,

- The Espionage Act of 1917 and its amended version, sometimes referred to as the Sedition Act of 1918, initiated by Woodrow Wilson, and

- The USA Patriot Act of 2001, initiated by George W. Bush

Each of these acts was ostensibly passed to enable administrations to better serve and protect the United States and its citizenry in times of danger. Effectively, however, each act made it possible for administrations to act without resistance or opposition. They accomplished that goal, in part, by severely restricting the scope and breath of information available to the public.

We have already addressed some of the negative affects of the Patriot Act, so lets look now at the Espionage Act of 1917 and the Sedition Act of 1918 during the Wilson administration.

Wilson became president of the United States in 1913—the year before World War I began. Most historical accounts maintain that Wilson, at least initially, tried to keep the United States out of the war, but others claim he intentionally, covertly maneuvered us into war. One way or the other, by April 1917, the United States was at war with Germany, and Wilson was devoting all of his and our country's energies and resources to the war effort. Part of that effort included a comprehensive campaign of deception and indoctrination that was facilitated by the Espionage Act of 1917 and the Sedition Act of 1918.

In preparation for war, Wilson understandably ordered a massive buildup of troops. Unfortunately, US military bases at that time were not equipped to handle them, so soldiers were forced to live in overcrowded, poorly heated, unsanitary conditions that, tragically, were ideal for the inception and spread of communicable diseases.

On March 4, 1918, influenza broke out at Fort Riley, Kansas. From there—primarily because troops were moved from base to base instead of quarantined—it quickly spread to other military bases, then to cities adjacent to those bases, and eventually on to France when US troops were deployed to fight there. This initiated a pandemic that eventually killed an estimated fifty million people worldwide (far more than all of the causalities from fighting during World War I)!

The influenza outbreak arguably posed a much greater threat to this country than Germany did, but Wilson was so consumed with the war effort that *he never even publicly acknowledged its existence!* In fact, in an attempt to maintain public morale, reporting agencies were ordered to play down its seriousness (Barry 2005).

Between 1918 and 1919, more than 550,000 Americans died from influenza. A great many of whom assumedly perished unnecessarily because reporting agencies were not allowed to inform the public regarding its severity.

Leaders in governments frequently insist that restricting public access to information is sometimes necessary. But a strong case can be made that restricting public access to pertinent, accurate information is never in society's best interests.

CORPORATE INTERVENTION

The risks associated with governmental intervention of free speech are significant, but the risks from corporate intervention today are arguably even greater. Most of the major reporting agencies are now owned, or otherwise influenced, by corporations that maintain very biased perspectives. For that reason, the media cannot be relied upon to regularly present accurate or even credible information.

An important consideration when evaluating the credibility of reported information is determining who owns or controls reporting agencies and what their motives are. It should come as no surprise that corporations do not magnanimously purchase reporting agencies so that they can provide pertinent information to the public. Their goals are to advance their own positions, and if they can accomplish those goals through deception and/ or indoctrination, they generally will.

Much of the information provided by the media is credible. But reporting agencies regularly disseminate misinformation as "news commentary" that inevitably reflects the sociopolitical ideologies of the corporations that own them. A case in point is Fox News. It is owned by the Fox Entertainment Group, a subsidiary of News Corporation.

Fox News debuted in 1996 when News Corporation founder, chairman, and chief executive officer Rupert Murdoch launched it as a cable news network. Its motto is: "Fair and Balanced News," which it most certainly is not. The opinions and commentary offered by Fox News are generally so ideologically **conservative** that they can only be regarded as political dogma. Its primary objective is to promote conservative ideologies and Republican candidates—not to inform audiences.

Their success is partially due to the fact that Fox News reporters and audiences have been thoroughly indoctrinated to believe that *their* ideologies are "right" and that all other ideologies are "wrong."

Our capacity to behave responsibly is dependent upon our ability to make objective decisions, and our ability to make objective decisions, to a large degree, is dependent upon our access to accurate information. Unfortunately, our primary sources of information today are reporting agencies that are owned by a very few corporations that are controlled by a very few individuals whose motives are to generate profits for their corporations. These are definitely not conditions conducive to the dissemination of accurate information.

Additionally, it is worth remembering that ignorance is a state of awareness resulting from *not* assimilating accurate information. Consequently, corporations can, and do, encourage public ignorance by *not* providing them with pertinent information. Nowhere are we likely to hear or read, for example, that over the past twenty-four hours more than two hundred thousand babies were born, mostly to parents who cannot afford to take care of them; or that forty thousand more acres of primary forest were cut down, mostly to grow soybeans, to feed cattle, to feed us; or that artificial development was responsible for the extinction of another 150–200 plant and animal species.

This type of information is critically important to the state of civilization, but it is not generally reported. While we allow ourselves to be distracted by relatively inconsequential and inane issues, our chances for saving civilization are slipping away.

This leads to an important question, just how much influence can one individual like Rupert Murdoch have on public opinion and behavior? Actually, an astounding amount. According to a 2006 press release, News Corporation was:

> a diversified international media and entertainment
> company with operations in eight industry segments: filmed
> entertainment; television; cable network programming; direct
> broadcast satellite television; magazines and inserts; newspapers;
> book publishing; and other…in the United States, Continental
> Europe, the United Kingdom, Australia, Asia and the Pacific
> Basin.[11]

As of 2005, News Corporation owned one hundred cable channels, forty television stations, nine satellite networks, 175 newspapers, forty book publishing imprints, and one movie studio—including Fox News Channel, Fox Business Network, the *New York Post*, the *Wall Street Journal*, *Barron's*, and HarperCollins Publishers.[12] In 2005, News Corporation's various media organizations reached 4.7 billion people worldwide (Kitty and Greenwald 2005, 49). Consequently, individuals like Murdoch have the capacity to profoundly influence world opinion and behavior.

11 http://www.newscorp.com/news/news_317.html
12 http://www.cjr.org/resources/?c=newscorp

At the present time, there are *no* reporting agencies that can be trusted to consistently provide accurate, comprehensive, pertinent information. But some sources are much better than others, and it is important that we learn to recognize and support them.

At the top of the list are public communication services, such as PBS (Public Broadcasting Service) and NPR (National Public Radio). Their programming is not completely free from corporate sponsorship, but the majority of their funding comes from public donations, so they are freer than most agencies to report objectively.

There are also independent reporting agencies that are worth mentioning. Most notable is Democracy Now!, which is actively and successfully practicing objective, but not necessarily comprehensive, journalism. According to their website, they are funded entirely through contributions from listeners, viewers, and foundations. They do not accept advertisers, corporate underwriters, or government funding, which allows them to exercise greater objectivity.

Additionally, a great deal of important, but generally unreported, information is made available through PBS special broadcasts (such as *Nova* and *Frontline*), National Geographic Explorer, and to a lesser degree, the History Channel. These broadcasts are not always completely accurate or comprehensive, but most of them make an honest attempt to present credible, pertinent information.

Reporting agencies are potentially valuable sources of accurate information, but as long as they are owned or controlled by corporations, they cannot be trusted to provide it. If we continue to rely on them as our primary sources of information, we will remain chronically under-informed, deceived, or deluded.

BOOKS AND SCHOLARLY ARTICLES

Books and scholarly articles have been one of our primary sources of credible information for hundreds of years. A great deal more effort is required to produce them than news articles, so they are generally regarded as *more* credible. But it is important to realize that *all* authors are subject to the same cultural foibles as parents, teachers, clerics, reporters, and everyone else when conveying information. Regardless of the subject matter, they will generally express biased viewpoints regarding them. It is a rare author indeed who can address a subject with complete objectivity.

In an effort to encourage accuracy and objectivity in professional books and scholarly articles, a peer review system was established. Peer review is a vetting process where an author's work, research, or ideas are subjected to the scrutiny of his peers who are experts in the field. The purpose of peer review is to ensure that authors meet accepted guidelines within their disciplines. The process has become so prevalent today among scholars and professionals that they will typically, arbitrarily dismiss publications (such as this one) simply because they have not been peer reviewed.

There is no doubt that the process does help to establish certain standards within scientific disciplines, but it also inhibits the expression of creative and/or independent thoughts. When innovative ideas occur to authors, they may not voice them for fear of criticism or rejection. It is important to realize that peer reviewers have also assimilated disinformation and dogma throughout their lives. This means that their opinions are biased and their abilities to review issues objectively are diminished.

Nevertheless, books and scholarly articles are important sources of reliable information that offer nearly unlimited potential for increasing awareness.

INTERNET

The Internet is fast becoming our most important source of information. Finding accurate information there can be difficult at times. But with few exceptions, no matter how obscure the subject is, with patience, reliable information regarding it can usually be found there.

One of the criticisms of information available on the Internet—especially by scholars and professionals—is that it is not peer reviewed. Certainly, there is a lot of misinformation and disinformation on the Internet, but as we have seen, there is *no* source that is completely reliable. The key to finding credible information on the Internet is to evaluate it objectively—just like with every other source of information.

COLLABORATIVE SITES

Currently, it is not regarded as acceptable to reference collaborative Internet sites such as Wikipedia. This is unfortunate, because Wikipedia, in particular, is generally as accurate, far more informative, and definitely more accessible than many respected academic sites.

It is imprudent to arbitrarily dismiss collaborative sources of information, because when carefully vetted, they can be as accurate or more accurate than peer reviewed sources. Collaboration also helps to ensure that information is current.

Despite present prejudices against collaborative sites, there will no doubt be a time in the not-too-distant future when carefully vetted collaborative sites, like Wikipedia, will be regarded as both reliable and citable.

Wikipedia was founded in 2001 by Jimmy Wales and Larry Sanger. According to their website:

> Wikipedia is a multilingual, web-based, free-content
> encyclopedia project based on an openly editable model....
> Wikipedia is written collaboratively by largely anonymous
> Internet volunteers who write without pay. [Currently,] there
> are more than 82,000 active contributors working on more
> than 19,000,000 articles in more than 270 languages....
> [Whether a contribution is used] depends upon whether it fits
> within Wikipedia's policies, including being verifiable against a

published reliable source…[and that] many experienced editors are watching to help and ensure that edits are cumulative improvements.[13]

Another Internet site worth mentioning is Snopes.com, a website devoted solely to researching the credibility of information. According to their website:

> The snopes.com website was founded by Barbara and David Mikkelson in 1995 as an expression of their shared interest in researching urban legends. [That effort] has since grown into what is widely regarded by folklorists, journalists, and laypersons alike as one of the World Wide Web's essential resources.
>
> The snopes.com web site is (and always has been) a completely independent, self-sufficient entity wholly owned by its operators, Barbara and David Mikkelson, and funded through advertising revenues. Neither the site nor its operators has ever received monies from (or been engaged in any business or editorial relationship with) any sponsor, investor, partner, political party, religious group, business organization, government agency, or any other outside group or organization.[14]

Snopes began by researching urban legends, but it now addresses the credibility of all sorts of pertinent information. They provide a valuable public service, and their efforts should be commended.

Currently, the Internet is not regulated by governments and not owned or overly influenced by corporations. But governments are trying to figure

---

13 http://en.wikipedia.org/wiki/Wikipedia:About
14 http://www.snopes.com/info/aboutus.asp

out how to regulate it, and communications corporations are trying to figure out how to gain control of it. We must never allow that to happen.

Regardless of how we access information, it is imperative that we realize that the assimilation of disinformation and dogma does not lead to greater intellectual or spiritual awareness, and that it actually impedes positive development and our chances for achieving sustainability.

Part II: Becoming Civilized

The end of the human race will be that it eventually dies of civilization.

—Ralph Waldo Emerson

3: The Adoption of Agriculture

Today the world changes so quickly that in growing up we take leave not just of youth but of the world we were young in.

—Peter Medawar

For the first 160,000 years of our existence, our species advanced very little. Then, about 12,000 years ago, somewhere along the Tigris and Euphrates Rivers in what is today southern Iraq, our foraging ancestors did something truly remarkable. They began to develop and adopt an alternative subsistence strategy, **agriculture.**

*In this discussion, the transition between foraging and agricultural subsistence strategies will be regarded as the threshold between essentially primitive or natural and essentially civilized or **artificial** existence. Furthermore, development that occurred before the adoption of agriculture will be regarded as natural and development that occurred after its adoption will be regarded as artificial.*

We will never know exactly what motivated our ancestors to develop agriculture and adopt it as their primary subsistence strategy. However it is quite likely that as they moved into temperate zones, they found it increasingly difficult to forage and store enough food to sustain them through unproductive winter seasons.

This would have been sufficient reason for them to experiment with additional and/or alternative subsistence strategies. Whatever their motive was for developing agriculture, however, it almost certainly stemmed from a need or desire to enhance their survival security.

The archaeological record suggests that agriculture[15] was adopted abruptly, but that scenario is extremely unlikely. "Foragers" almost certainly practiced limited agriculture for thousands of years by broadcasting seeds of favored edible plants in opportune locations, weeding out competing plant species, constructing barriers to protect *their* crops from wild animals, and other activities that left no evidence of their existence. It wasn't "foragers" became sedentary and adopted agriculture as their *primary* subsistence strategy that durable evidence of agriculture was produced.

It is no coincidence that agriculture was first developed and adopted in the Middle East. There were more domesticable wild plant species there (wheat, barley, lentil, broad bean, onion, walnut, pomegranate, grape, fig, date, apricot, olive, etc.) and animal species (oxen, horse, donkey, sheep, goat, camel, etc.) than anywhere else on Earth. It is also no coincidence that agriculture began there when it did. At that time, in that region, climatic conditions were uncharacteristically favorable for its inception. The most important consideration regarding the development and adoption of agriculture, however, is that it was completely voluntary. For the first, and perhaps only, time in Earth's history, a species consciously decided to develop and adopt an alternative subsistence strategy.

Initially, agriculture could only be practiced where there was sufficient rainfall to support it. Within just a few thousand years of its inception, however, our clever ancestors learned to divert water from rivers and streams so that they could irrigate crops and thus practice agriculture in more arid regions. At that time, agricultural communities began to appear all along the major and minor river valleys in the Middle East.

---

15 Agriculture was developed independently in a number of areas, but it was first practiced in the Middle East, and the agricultural model that was established there is the one that has prevailed. Consequently, it alone will be addressed in this discussion.

ARTIFICIAL DEVELOPMENT

The adoption of agriculture and sedentary existence in conjunction with our innate abilities to conceptualize and communicate opened the door for rampant artificial development. Artificial development gave us the power to exert our will over other species and the environment. In effect, it enabled us to circumvent, at least temporarily, *natural* selection and replace it with what can best be regarded as *artificial* selection. In a relatively short period of time, artificial development enabled us to become the dominant mammal species on Earth—by a substantial margin.

ANTHROPOCENTRISM

This newfound power could have instilled a sense of humility in our species, but it did not. Instead, it made us extremely arrogant and **centric**. We cannot know how our foraging ancestors regarded other species and the environment, but more contemporaneous foragers universally regarded them with a level of respect bordering on reverence. Once our ancestors became civilized, however, they began to regard only exploitable species and environments as valuable and worth preserving. Those that were not regarded as immediately exploitable, were generally deemed worthless and expendable.

Anthropocentrism may have facilitated our rapid ascension into civilization, but much of the irresponsible, insensitive, and unconscionable behavior that we exhibit can be attributed to it. Unfortunately, we tend to overlook the negative aspects of anthropocentrism, because we have profited enormously from it—at least so far.

Nevertheless, we are at least subconsciously aware that our behavior towards other species and the environment is shameful. In fact, a strong argument can be made that shame is what initially prompted our ancestors to create gods who not only condoned anthropocentric behavior, but advocated it.

This must have been a matter of concern by at least 3,300 years ago, because it was one of the first issues addressed in Genesis:

> And God said: "Let us make man in our image, after our likeness. They shall rule the fish of the sea, the birds of the sky, the cattle, the whole earth, and all the creeping things that creep on the earth." (Genesis 1:26)

> The fear and the dread of you shall be upon all the beasts of the earth, and upon all the birds of the sky—everything with which the earth is astir—and upon the fish of the sea; they are given into your hand. (Genesis 9:2)

AGRO-CENTRISM

Utilizing similar centric attitudes, civilized people (agriculturalists) have always regarded primitive people (foragers) as inferior and therefore expendable. Regarding that attitude, Charles Darwin once noted:

> At some future period, not very distant as measured by centuries, the civilized races of man will almost certainly exterminate and replace the savage races throughout the world.

As it turns out, agriculture and foraging are not compatible subsistence strategies and cannot coexist on the same landscape. The dynamics of agriculture are simply too exploitive. They require exclusive use of the most productive land, the damming and diversion of watercourses, the extermination of competing species, and many other activities that diminish the natural carrying capacities of land to support foragers.

It is impossible to know how foragers and agriculturalists initially reacted to each other. However, soon after the adoption of agriculture, conflicts between them began that lasted until agriculturalists eventually vanquished, as Darwin predicted, every foraging society on Earth. He erred only in the length of time that it would take for civilized man to accomplish that task.

Our successful application of artificial development seems to justify the centric beliefs we maintain about ourselves. However, they encourage irresponsible, and in many cases, unconscionable behavior that adversely affects other members of our species, other species, and the environment. If we continue to allow centric beliefs to influence our behavior, our tenure as civilized beings on Earth will inevitably end ignominiously in the not-too-distant future.

It is essential that we realize that behavior that was appropriate in natural states of existence is not necessarily appropriate in civilized states of existence, and that only by modifying our behavior can we achieve sustainability.

IRRESPONSIBLE AGRICULTURAL PRACTICES

One of the biggest concerns regarding artificial development should be the establishment of responsible, sustainable agriculture. Our survival and the fate of civilization depends completely on it, and yet we are allowing its practice to be motivated completely by profit—hardly the best way to encourage responsible behavior. Nothing can illustrate this issue more clearly than by examining the leading US agricultural company, Monsanto.

MONSANTO

Monsanto was founded in 1901. According to its website, its role is "supporting farmers around the world in their mission to feed, clothe and fuel our growing world." Monsanto's statement of intent makes the company appear responsible and socially concerned, but that is definitely not the case. It has a very dark history as a toxic chemical producer and polluter, and its current stated goal is to gain control of the world's seed production, so that it can offer only genetically modified (GM) patented seeds provided by them.

Listed below is a synopsis (condensed from its website) of Monsanto's involvement in the agricultural industry since 1964:[16]

Monsanto develops and introduces the following herbicides:

1964 - Ramrod
1968 - Lasso
1976 - Roundup

Monsanto begins to focus its energies on molecular biology with the development of:

1975 - Cell biology research program
1981 - Molecular biology group
1982 - First genetic modification of a plant cell
1994 - First biotechnology product to win regulatory approval, **Posilac**

Monsanto introduces genetically modified seed varieties resistant to its Roundup herbicide:

1996 - Roundup Ready Soybeans
1997 - Roundup Ready Canola
1997 - Roundup Ready Cotton
1997 - Roundup Ready Corn

Monsanto begins to acquire biotech research companies:

1996 - Agracetus
1996 - Calgene
1998 - DeKalb Genetics Corp.
2004 - Channel Bio Corp. (by Monsanto's ASI)

---

16 http://www.monsanto.com/who_we_are/history.asp

Monsanto introduces another genetically modified seed variety resistant to its Roundup herbicide

2006 - Roundup Ready Flex Cotton

Monsanto acquires the following seed companies:

1996 - Asgrow agronomics seed industry
1997 - Holden's Foundation Seeds, LLC
1997 - Corn States Hybrid Service, LLC (corn seed supplier)
1997 - Jacob Hartz Seed Co. (soybean seed supplier)
2004 - American Seeds, Inc., ASI (formed by Monsanto)
2004 - Crows Hybrid Corn
2004 - Midwest Seed Genetics
2004 - Wilson Seeds
2005 - Seminis, Inc.
2005 - Stoneville cotton industry (including its NexGen brand)

Monsanto's ASI subsidiary acquires:

2005 - NC+ Hybrids, Inc.
2005 - Fontanelle Hybrids
2005 - Stewart Seeds
2005 - Trelay Seeds
2005 - Stone Seeds (all shareowners of the CORE Group)
2005 - Specialty Hybrids (corn seed supplier)

After the development of Roundup herbicide in 1976, Monsanto began developing GM crops that were resistant to it, so that those crops could be sprayed with Roundup after they germinated to kill weeds without harming the crops.

It also began to buy up seed companies, so that it could control the varieties of seeds made available to farmers. Not surprisingly, Monsanto offers only genetically modified seed varieties that are "Roundup Ready." Consequently, farmers have little choice but to plant GM crops and use

Roundup herbicide. The agricultural industry is now committed to this approach. According to the June 2008 Monthly Update, "Genetically Modified Crops and the Future of World Agriculture,"[17] the percentage of GM plantings is increasing rapidly (fig. 1). Since Monsanto currently produces between 70 and 100 percent of GM seeds, its share in the world market is enormous.

	Soybeans %	Corn %	Cotton %	Canola %
United States	93	52	79	82
Canada	60	65	–	95
Argentina	99	62	50	–
South Africa	65	27	95	–
Australia	–	–	90	–
China	–	–	65	–
Brazil	40	–	–	–
Uruguay	100	–	–	–

Figure 1: GM percentage of crop plantings in 2005

GENETIC MODIFICATION

Genetic engineering is a laboratory procedure used to modify DNA (deoxyribonucleic acid) in living organisms. DNA provides the genetic instructions used in the development and maintenance of all living organisms. These instructions manifest themselves as genetic coding, different in each individual. Variability is a crucial aspect of a species' long-term survival, because it ensures genetic diversity.

---

17 http://earthtrends.wri.org/updates/node/313

Molecular biologists have discovered how to modify DNA using enzymes and viral vectors to alter its characteristics. Today, biologists take genes out of fish, for example, and introduce them into tomatoes to extend the tomatoes' growing season. The potential for this type of technology must be very exciting to researchers, but these engineers are artificially, genetically modifying organisms that evolved over many millions of years—the ramifications of which are very disturbing and potentially catastrophic.

Genetically modified crops have not been around long enough for potential problems to manifest themselves. As for their impact on human health, researchers are particularly concerned that they may cause allergies or cancer. If past experiences with such experimental developments are any indications of what to expect, their concerns are justified—*there will be unanticipated problems.*

Recently, for example, scientists from Cornell University discovered that genetically modified corn pollen, when it lands on neighboring milkweed plants, is extremely toxic to monarch butterfly caterpillars.[18] This may seem like a small price to pay for increased crop production, but there will undoubtedly be other adverse effects associated with GM crops that we are not aware of yet—some of which may be far more serious.

GOVERNMENT SAFEGUARDS?

One would think that regulatory agencies like the US Department of Agriculture (USDA) and the Food and Drug Administration (FDA) would insist on comprehensive testing before GM crops were grown extensively, or products made from them were offered to the public. After all, these crops and products are not natural, so we have no idea what effects they may have on the environment or us. Disturbingly, that is not the case. The FDA's 1992 policy statement granted GM foods GRAS (generally

---

18 http://www.commondreams.org/views01/0628-01.htm

recognized as safe) status. That position was upheld in June 2009, when the FDA stated:

> Committee members also suggested that we develop a more expedited process for FDA and the industry to reach decisions on the marketing of other bioengineered foods that do not raise substantive scientific issues.

> Subsequently, the FDA established an informal process by which firms can inform the agency that they have completed a food or feed safety assessment. The FDA requests that firms submit to the agency a summary of their assessment. It is our expectation and experience that all firms have complied with this request for all plant varieties that have been commercialized to date. This process has worked well to date and permits the agency to identify and resolve any safety or regulatory issues before products reach the market.[19]

In other words, the FDA expects the companies that manufacture GM crops to determine whether they are safe or not. This is particularly alarming in light of a statement made by Phil Angell, Monsanto's director of corporate communications:

> Monsanto should not have to vouchsafe the safety of biotech food. Our interest is in selling as much of it as possible. Assuring its safety is the FDA's job.[20]

Ten years ago, there were no products in US supermarkets that contained GM crops. Today, about 70 percent of them do.[21] According to Martin A. Lee:

---

19 http://biotechgmfoods.blogspot.com/

20 http://www.sourcewatch.org/index.php?title=Philip_Angell (quoting from *New York Times Magazine*, October 25, 1998)

21 http://www.realfooddigest.com/2011/01/how-to-avoid-dangerous-genetically-modified-foods/

[The FDA] acknowledges that it has been operating under an explicit government policy "to foster" the biotechnology industry since 1992. That year, the FDA declared GE (genetically engineered) foods to be "substantially equivalent" to normal foods and, therefore, exempt from special pre-market testing—a determination that many of the FDA's own scientists strongly disagreed with.[22]

DISCLOSURE

In 1992, the FDA also addressed mandatory labeling of foods made from GM crops. The agency determined that foods made from GM crops did not differ from other foods in any significant way, and that the procedures used to create them presented no greater safety concerns than foods developed by traditional plant-breeding methods. Consequently, mandatory labeling was not required.[23]

This means that the public has no choice but to consume foods containing GM crops. If the FDA required that they be labeled, the public could at least avoid them if they wanted to. But most elected officials in the government received sizable campaign contributions from agribusiness, so their primary loyalties are to them, not to us. The net affect of this is that the US government, at all levels, is allowing agribusiness to do whatever they want. And agribusiness wants to make a lot of money—regardless of the costs to us, other species, or the environment.

MAINTAINING GENETIC DIVERSITY

The greatest risk associated the GM crop production, however, is arguably its adverse affects on genetic diversity. Since the development of agriculture, farmers have meticulously saved the best of their seeds for replanting the

---

22 http://www.commondreams.org/views01/0628-01.htm

23 http://ncseonline.org/nle/crsreports/agriculture/ag-98.cfm

following year. This tradition helped to develop and maintain genetic diversity within crop varieties. Unfortunately, it is a tradition that is on the wane.

Pollen from genetically modified strains can, and does, cross-pollinate with genetically natural strains. Farmers who have saved seed for years, decades, or even generations are finding that their crops are becoming contaminated with GM strains. Astoundingly, when Monsanto realized this, it began to sue farmers for patent infringement! As of February, 2012 they had brought suit against more than eight hundred small farmers, and thus far have not lost a single case.[24]

Because of this, farmers in many areas will no longer risk saving and planting their own seed. They cannot afford to fight Agi-monsters like Monsanto. Ironically, if they want to stay in business, they have to buy seed from them! This, of course is what Monsanto and other seed producers want, but it is eliminating genetic diversity from many crop species.

When companies such as Monsanto develop GM seed varieties, they typically offer *only* those varieties. Monsanto controls about 85 percent of the seed market in the United States. This means that approximately 79 percent of the soybean plants, 44 percent of the corn plants, 67 percent of the cotton plants, and 70 percent of the canola plants grown here are *genetically identical.* This strategy may be very lucrative for Monsanto, but it is also extremely risky. If a pervasive fungus or disease attacks one of those crops, it could wipe out the entire crop.

This happened in Europe in the mid 1800's. At that time, farmers planted a single variety of potato known as the "lumper."[25] Potato varieties are propagated vegetatively, so individual plants within each variety are genetically identical to each other.

Beginning in 1845, a fungus outbreak known as "the blight" spread through potato crops all across Europe, reducing harvests by as much as 100 percent in some areas. The blight was particularly devastating because

---

24 http://www.cornucopia.org/2012/02/judge-sides-with-monsanto-in-lawsuit/
25 http://evolution.berkeley.edu/evolibrary/article//agriculture_02

all of the plants exposed to it were genetically identical to each other and therefore, equally susceptible to it.

The potato blight presented difficulties throughout Europe, but nowhere more so than in Ireland, where it caused what would later be known as the Great Famine. Between 1845 and 1855 Ireland lost between 20 and 25 percent of its population—partly due to starvation and partly due to migration.

Avoiding such catastrophes requires maintaining significant genetic diversity within crop varieties, but uniformity is more profitable than diversity in modern agriculture, so that is the direction it is headed. This trend needs to be reversed, but it will be difficult. Even if seed suppliers decided to offer diverse strains of seeds, they would not be able to—at least not immediately. Gene banks, such as the famous Svalbard Global Seed Vault in Norway, heirloom seed companies, and concerned individuals maintain thousands of varieties of genetically diverse seeds—but not in commercial quantities. It would take many years to reestablish genetic diversity throughout the world's crops.

ROUNDUP HERBICIDE

Genetically modified crops are designed to be used in conjunction with glyphosate herbicides. Glyphosate is a non-selective, broad-spectrum poison that was developed by Monsanto in 1970 and brought to market by them under the brand name Roundup in 1976.

Roundup kills by traveling along what are called shikimate, metabolic pathways that exist in plant—but not animal species. Because animal species do not have these pathways, they cannot metabolize glyphosate and cannot be poisoned by it. This does not mean, however, that glyphosate will not *harm* animal species if they are exposed to it. It definitely will, but the reasons for that are complex and not readily apparent.

Until quite recently, researchers believed that animal species were capable of making all of the enzymes they needed to convert food into energy and to use it to repair tissues and organs—but that is not the case. Each animal organism is actually dependent upon trillions of microorganisms to carryout basic physiological processes. As it turns out, they (we) cannot survive without them.

Unfortunately, microorganisms also have shikimate pathways and are extremely susceptible to glyphosate poisoning—a fact that researchers failed to recognize when evaluating its risks. The implications of glyphosate-microorganism-poisoning *in* animal species (us) is just beginning to be recognized. However, an article recently published in the journal *Entropy* stated that glyphosate herbicides are possibly:

> the most important factor in the development of multiple
> chronic diseases and conditions that have become prevalent in
> Westernized societies.

Additionally, according to Dr. Stephanie Seneff PhD there are now positive correlations between glyphosate-microorganism- poisoning in humans and increasing occurrences of autism, inflammatory bowel disease, chronic diarrhea, colitis, Crohn's disease, obesity, cardiovascular disease, depression, cancer, cachexia, Alzheimer's disease, Parkinson's disease, multiple sclerosis, and others.[26]

Glyphosate herbicides are also assumedly damaging and/or destroying microorganisms in Earth's soil—the negative affects of which are presently unknown, but could be truly devastating. It is after all, soil bacteria that enables plants to grow in the first place.

CORRUPTION

The USDA and the FDA have chosen not to regulate GM crops—and not to support mandatory labeling of them. This is an indication that their loyalties lie with agribusinesses (like Monsanto) that produce GM crops and products—not with the public. Monsanto has powerful lobbies in

26 http://responsibletechnology.org titled Monsanto's Roundup Herbicide

Washington, DC, but there is another reason it has not been subjected to even minimal regulations. It is powerful enough to get its employees influential positions in the federal government. For example:[27]

- Margaret Miller, deputy director of the FDA, was previously one of Monsanto's top scientists, developing recombinant bovine growth hormones (**rBGH**).

- Clarence Thomas, Supreme Court justice (who cast the deciding vote in 2000, giving the presidency to George W. Bush), was previously an attorney for Monsanto.

- Michael Taylor, deputy commissioner for policy of the FDA (a role created to expedite the approval process of genetically engineered foods), was previously an attorney for Monsanto. (Taylor later became vice president of Monsanto).

- Rufus Yerxa, US Deputy to the World Trade Organization, was previously chief counsel for Monsanto.

- Michael Kantor, US Secretary of Commerce, was previously on the board of directors of Monsanto.

- Carol Tucker Foreman, the sole "consumer advocate" on an international committee assessing genetically modified foods, was previously a lobbyist for Monsanto.

- Anne Veneman, US Secretary of Agriculture (whose role was, among other things, to regulate genetically engineered crops), was previously on the board of directors of Calgene (a Monsanto biotech subsidiary).

---

27 http://www.occupymonsanto360.org/Occupy,Monsanto,GMO,Genetic,Engineering,Modified,Organism,Food,Sustainable,Local,Locavore,Organic,RoundUp/michael-taylor/

- Donald Rumsfeld, US Secretary of Defense, was previously the CEO of the Searle pharmaceutical corporation, acquired by Monsanto.

- Linda Fisher, deputy administrator of the US Environmental Protection Agency, was previously Monsanto's vice president of government affairs.

All of these positions represent conflicts of interest. Margaret Miller's primary project at Monsanto, for example, was the development of the genetically engineered growth hormone rBGH. Appallingly, her first act as deputy director of the FDA was to approve that drug.

These positions were presidential appointments made by George H. W. Bush, Bill Clinton, and George W. Bush. Unfortunately, Monsanto's influence did not end there. Despite campaign promises to the contrary, President Obama has selected his agricultural leaders directly from the ranks of Monsanto, DuPont, and the other pesticide and genetic engineering companies:[28]

- Michal Taylor, deputy commissioner for foods of the FDA, was previously the vice president of Monsanto.

- Roger Beachy, director of the USDA National Institute of Food and Agriculture, was previously a director of the Monsanto-funded Danforth Plant Science Center.

- Islam Siddiqui, agriculture negotiator for the US Trade Representative, was previously vice president of the Monsanto and Dupont funded, pesticide-promoting lobbyist group CropLife.

- Rajiv Shah, USDA undersecretary for research education and economics as well as chief scientist and who is now head of

---

28 http://www.organicconsumers.org/usda_watch.cfm#vilsack

USAID, was previously the agricultural development director for the pro-biotech Gates Foundation (a frequent Monsanto partner).

- Elena Kagan, President Obama's solicitor general, took Monsanto's side against organic farmers in the Roundup Ready alfalfa case.

- Ramona Romero, nominated by President Obama to serve as general counsel for the USDA, was previously corporate counsel to DuPont.

Why US presidents appointed corporate personnel into important, high-level government positions when there were clearly conflicts of interest with them is not known. However, it is safe to assume that for one reason or another, they owed those corporations "favors."

Monsanto is desperately trying to convince the world that biotechnology is the answer to tomorrow's agricultural problems, and that we should trust them to lead the way with this new technology. But common sense and a preponderance of evidence suggests that biotechnology is not the answer, and that Monsanto cannot be trusted to provide it (see Chapter 11: Pollution). In fact, Monsanto is a self-serving corporation that poses serious risks to the long-term best interests of our species. One cannot research any aspect of Monsanto without uncovering damning and disturbing information about their irresponsible behavior: from the production, careless use, and disposal of toxic chemicals to issues surrounding genetic engineering and the strong-arm tactics they employ against farmers who resist using their products.

Monsanto is determined to transform agriculture into vast stands of patented, genetically identical, GM crops—even though it threatens global food security, and the vast majority of consumers worldwide are opposed to it. Monsanto may be powerful enough to control "our" government, but it is not powerful enough to control an *aware* and *proactive* public. This is an important distinction, because only we can bring about meaning-ful change (see Chapter 17: Practice Responsible Agriculture). In 2001, Martin A. Lee wrote in the *San Francisco Bay Guardian*:[29]

> Resistance to biotechnology is growing, particularly in poor countries such as India, where several experimental GE [GM] plots were set on fire during a "Cremate Monsanto" campaign waged by an association of 10 million landless peasants. The Landless Workers' Movement[30] in Brazil has made stopping Monsanto soybeans a top priority. And farmers in Thailand have taken a strong stand against genetic engineering while participating in a "Long March for Biodiversity."
>
> In 1999, anti-biotech activists destroyed all the field trials of genetically modified trees in England, and protesters have staged similar actions in France and elsewhere. Bioengineered products are unpopular in Europe, and grassroots opposition is strong throughout the continent. The seeds of a consumer revolt have also taken root in the United States, where support for biotechnology is eroding, according to recent public opinion polls. By an overwhelming majority, Americans favor the mandatory labeling of GE foods.

INDOCTRINATION CAMPAIGN

In response to public resistance to GM foods and their mandatory labeling, the Council for Biotechnology Information was established. According to their website,[31] its members are the "leading agricultural biotechnical

---

29 http://www.commondreams.org/views01/0628-01.htm

30 The Landless Workers' Movement is the largest social movement in Latin America.

31 http://www.whybiotech.com/about/members.asp#1

companies"[32] and its purpose is to communicate "science-based information about the benefits and safety of agricultural biotechnology and its contributions to sustainable development." Apparently, communicating "science-based information" includes deceiving and indoctrinating children. *The Biotechnology Basics Activity Book* circulated to children is an example of this approach. It begins:

Hi Kids,

Welcome to the Biotechnology Basics Activity Book.[33]
This is an activity book for young people like you about
biotechnology—a really neat topic. Why is it such a neat
topic? Because biotechnology is helping to improve the health
of the earth and the people who call it home. In this book,
you will take a closer look at biotechnology. You will see that
biotechnology is being used to figure out how to: 1) grow more
food; 2) help the environment; and 3) grow more nutritious
food that improves our health. As you work through the puzzles
in this book, you will learn more about biotechnology and all
of the wonderful ways it can help people live better lives in a
healthier world.

Have fun!

FUTURE

In light of all we know regarding the risks of GM crops, it would be prudent to phase them out over the next ten years—not only in this country but worldwide. In the meantime, all foods containing GM crops should be

---

32 BASF Plant Science, Bayer CropScience, Dow AgroServices LLC, Dupont, *Monsanto,*
   and Syngenta

33 http://www.whybiotech.com/resources/Kids-Biotech-Basics-Activity-Book.pdf

labeled as such so that people can avoid them if they choose (see Chapter 17: Practice Responsible Agriculture).

Unfortunately, the pressure to grow more food is intense. On June 3, 2008, at the High-level Conference on World Food Security in Rome, UN Secretary General Ban Ki-Moon stated:

> The world needs to produce more food. Food production needs to rise by 50 percent by the year 2030 to meet the rising demand.[34]

Agribusiness argues that GM crops are the only way this need can be met. But the solution to world hunger is not to feed increasingly more people with unsustainable agricultural practices. It is to lower our population (see Chapter 25: Reduce Our Population).

OVERPOPULATION

Another major concern regarding artificial development is that it enables rampant population growth. Initially, population growth helped to ensure the maintenance of our societies and the perpetuation of our species, but that is no longer the case. Our population long ago exceeded an optimum, sustainable level, and yet we continue to allow it to grow. To put population growth in perspective, it is currently increasing more *every week* than it did in the first 130,000 years of human existence (fig. 2).

We tend to regard rampant population growth as evidence of our successful application of artificial development and our species' superiority. But allowing our population to continue to grow unchecked is incredibly irresponsible and is not—or is no longer—in our best interests.

---

34 http://www.un.org/apps/sg/sgstats.asp?nid=3202

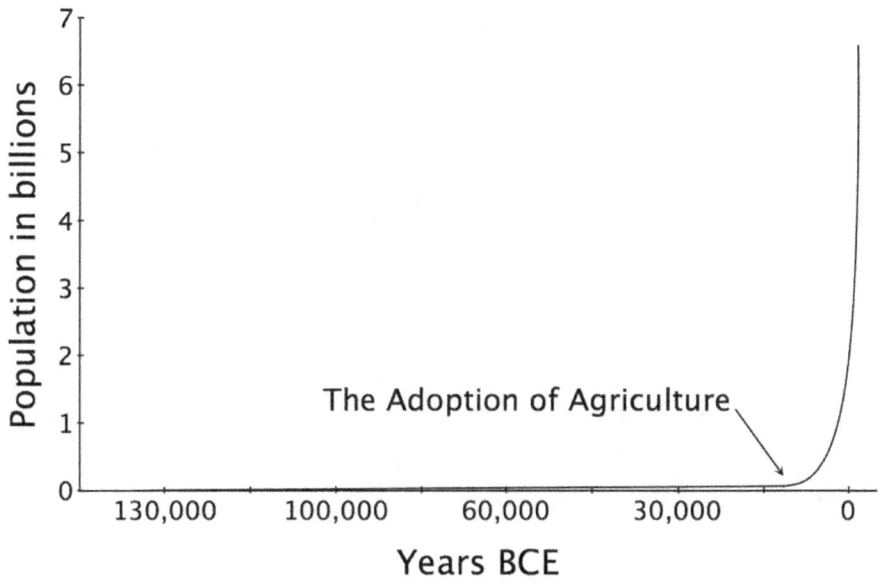

Figure 2: Population increase since the adoption of agriculture

Artificial development has enabled our population to increase, but it is the competitive nature of artificial development that has caused it to increase beyond sustainable levels. Utilizing competitive developmental strategies allows societies to grow large and powerful—but only for short periods of time. Excessive populations exacerbate nearly all of the chronic problems that threaten them: overcrowding, pollution, environmental degradation, loss of biota, resource depletion, etc. Consequently, excessive populations almost always eventually lead to societal collapse.

Encouraging, or even allowing unrestrained population growth to continue is not in our societies' or civilizations' best interests, but until recently, the short-term demands posed by inter-societal competition necessitated rampant population growth. Societies were far more concerned with their immediate survival needs than the long-term negative effects of overpopulation.

The correlation between competition and overpopulation represents a chronic problem associated with the current manifestation of artificial development and one that will have to be resolved if civilization is to continue (see Chapter 25: Reduce Our Population).

It is impossible to know exactly what *will* happen if we don't resolve these issues, but it is worth considering several possibilities.

FAMINE

According to the World Food Programme (WFP) website, 925 million people are malnourished in the world today.[35] That means that 14 percent of the world's population does not get enough food to lead healthy, productive lives. The WFP claims that malnutrition currently poses a greater risk to worldwide health than AIDS, malaria, and tuberculosis combined. Statistics vary as to how many people die each year from starvation, but even the most conservative estimates concede that at least seven million people, mostly children, die each year from famine.

Death tolls can be very much higher locally at times. For example:[36]

- Approximately one million people died during the Great Irish Famine between 1845–1855.

- Approximately eight million people died during the Russian famine of 1921.

- Approximately seven million people died during the Soviet Famine of 1932–1939.

- Approximately four million people died during the Bengal famine of 1943.

---

35 http://www.wfp.org/hunger

36 http://en.wikipedia.org/wiki/List_of_wars_and_anthropogenic_disasters_by_death_toll

- Approximately three million people died during the Vietnamese Famine of 1945.

- Approximately *thirty-five million* people died during the Great Chinese Famine between 1958–1962.

These are appallingly high numbers, but currently, starvation does not pose a serious risk to our species, civilization, or even individual societies. However, our ability to provide enough food to feed even our current population is dependent upon a great many variables we have no control over—especially climate. Researchers claim that climatic variations of only a few degrees could seriously upset our agricultural infrastructure. Those who are most optimistic predict that if global temperatures rise several degrees, agricultural activity will simply shift to higher latitudes in the Northern Hemisphere, lower latitudes in the Southern Hemisphere, and higher elevations in both hemispheres. But those models are based on the assumption that there is equal soil fertility and availability of water in those regions—which is not the case at all.

Besides the risks posed by climate change, we must also consider the increased risks of comprehensive crop failures due to irresponsible agricultural practices, such as planting genetically identical crops.

In any event, whether by natural or artificial causes, there may be a time in the not-too-distant future when farmers will not be able to produce as much food as they currently are. If the net loss of production is drastic or sudden and our population is excessive (which it already is), then the starvation rate could quickly rise from millions to billions. Having that many people die during a single famine would not threaten the integrity of our species, but it would certainly initiate the collapse of many modern societies and possibly even civilization itself.

DISEASE

The threat of famine is significant, but the risk of disease is even greater. Disease has the capacity to kill off large segments of populations in very short periods of time.

Species populations are controlled naturally by various combinations of predation, starvation, and disease through a process known as natural selection. Natural selection helps to maintain a balance in nature, but that does not mean species populations are always in balance. In fact, they seldom are. Species populations fluctuate—sometimes dramatically.

It is difficult to objectively assess the dynamics of our own population. This is primarily because artificial development is enabling us to circumvent natural selection through increased food production, health care, etc. There is no way of knowing how long we can get away with this. However, if we used artificial selection *only* to maintain a sustainable population, it is possible that we could get away with it indefinitely.

Unfortunately, we are allowing our population to greatly exceed Earth's natural capacity to sustain it. If we allow this trend to continue, when natural selection does eventually prevail—which it most certainly will—we will undoubtedly experience a monumental die-off; not because we angered God or Mother Nature, but because we carelessly primed ourselves for it.

PANDEMICS

Barring catastrophic natural events (such as meteor impacts and super volcanic eruptions), the greatest risk to civilization and humanity is posed by pandemics, and those risks are made increasingly more likely by overpopulation.

Pandemics are caused by viruses, but not all viruses are harmful. Those that are harmful are called pathogens, but most pathogens, like the common cold, are not particularly virulent. Some pathogens, however, are extremely deadly. Pandemics have been responsible for massive die-offs in the past (Giblin 1995):

- 541–750 CE: An estimated one hundred million people in Europe, Asia, and North Africa died from a pandemic thought to be bubonic plague. It killed approximately 50 to 60 percent of the population there in just eleven years.

- 1347–1352: The infamous Black Death pandemic killed approximately twenty-five million people in Europe, Asia, and North Africa. The mortality rate was 25 to 50 percent.

- 1492–1600: Europeans introduced smallpox, measles, typhus, and other diseases to isolated indigenous populations in the New World. From there they spread throughout North and South America eventually killing an estimated *one hundred million people*. The mortality rate in the New World is believed to have been close to 90 percent.

- 1556–1560: A deadly form of influenza surfaced in Europe that killed an estimated 20 percent of the population in 4 years.

- 1918–1919: the Great Influenza, or Spanish flu, pandemic killed between 25 and 50 million people worldwide in just 2 years.

It may seem unlikely that modern societies, such as our own, could be at serious risk from pathogens today, but that is not the case.

SUSCEPTIBILITY

According to the World Health Organization, AIDS has killed about twenty-five million people since it was first discovered in 1981. That is a lot of people, but when compared to the number of deaths caused by other pathogens in the past—*as a percentage of the population,* it is not. However, HIV is a very insidious disease, because it can be asymptomatic. This means that individuals can carry, and unknowingly transmit, AIDS for years before they are even aware they have it. Consequently, HIV is actually more prevalent than the statistics indicate. Currently, there are an estimated forty-two million additional people who are infected with the virus.[37]

As far as pathogens go, HIV is relatively difficult to transmit. It can only be spread through intimate contact between two individuals—typically sexually and through shared needles from intravenous drug use. Thus, another insidious aspect of the pathogen is that it is transmitted primarily through instinctive and addictive activities that are nearly impossible to curb or regulate. This is why, despite all of our efforts, HIV continues to spread.

HIV is a virulent pathogen, but because it is not easily transmitted, it does not pose a serious risk to humanity or even to civilization. Currently, there are about fourteen thousand new cases of HIV every day,[38] which on a global scale is not that many. However, if the HIV virus mutated into a strain that could be transmitted more readily—through insect bites or the air, for example—and it remained largely asymptomatic, the vast majority of humanity could be infected with it before we even knew there was a problem.

Something similar to that actually happened with the bubonic plague in Europe during the 1300s.[39] Initially, it was carried in rats and transmitted to humans through fleabites. The bubonic plague attacked the lymph nodes of its victims and usually killed them within a week. The virus then mutated into an airborne strain called pneumonic plague that attacked the respiratory systems of its victims. That strain could be contracted simply by inhaling the exhaled air of infected individuals and was far more virulent. It would generally kill its victims in less than two days.

No one knows for certain what initially caused the Black Death pandemic in the 1300s. Many researchers believe it originated in Tibet. There,

---

37 http://www.until.org/statistics.shtml

38 http://www.until.org/statistics.shtml

39 http://www.eyewitnesstohistory.com/plague.htm

deteriorating environmental conditions forced marmots out of their normal high-elevation ranges into lower elevations where they were in closer proximity to humans. That allowed **vectors** (such as fleas) to transfer the virus carried by the marmots to people. Marmots may or may not have been the cause for the Black Death pandemic in the fourteenth century, but they are chronic plague carriers and are known to have been responsible for a number of other less catastrophic plague epidemics in Asia since then.

Ascertaining the origins of pandemics is extremely difficult. For example, researchers have been diligently trying to determine the cause of the 1918–1919 influenza epidemic since the 1930s. Reliable evidence suggests that it originated in Haskell County, Kansas (Barry 2005), but there is no way to prove it. Nevertheless, nearly everyone agrees that it was a new viral strain of avian flu—not a recurring pathogen.[40] That new strain either crossed directly over to humans from birds or possibly first to pigs and then to humans. In any event, it was so easily transmitted that it quickly became a pandemic.

Most virulent pathogens are either viruses carried by wild animals that are not generally in contact with humans or are mutated viral strains carried by domestic animals that are in regular contact with humans. Humans are most often exposed to pathogens carried by wild animals as a result of deteriorating habitat conditions that force them into closer contact, such as with the aforementioned marmot migrations in Tibet.

Why viral mutations occur in domesticated animals is not clear. However, in their natural states, they roam freely and are accustomed to great diversity in their diets and general living conditions. Domestication forces them to live in confined, sedentary, overcrowded, and typically unsanitary conditions. It is not known for certain, but it is reasonable to assume that the degenerate conditions domestic animals are subjected to,

---

40 http://www.bytown.net/flu1918.htm

may cause, or at least provide greater opportunities for, viral mutations to occur.

Pandemics have struck devastating blows to regional human populations in the past. Global pandemics, however, are a modern phenomenon. Until recently, the spread of disease was restricted by the temporal and/or spatial limitations of human travel. The Bubonic plague pandemic of 1347, for example, took several years to spread from Asia to Europe and North Africa, because it was dependent on the spread of fleas carried directly and indirectly by pedestrian and equestrian human travel.[41] The bubonic plague did not spread to North America, South America, or Australia during the 1300s, because there was no human travel to those continents at that time.

By contrast, because of intra-continental train travel and trans-oceanic ship travel, the Spanish flu of 1918–1919 spread to almost every habited area on Earth in a very short period of time.

If a similar pandemic occurred today, with all of the international air travel that takes place, it is likely that somewhere between one hundred million and two hundred million people would die—most of them within thirty days. Its effects on humanity would be devastating, but most societies and civilization would probably survive. But if a pathogen as virulent as smallpox surfaced today, the death toll could conceivably be as high as *six billion*. If that happened, extensive inter-societal cooperation would undoubtedly cease, and civilization would end.

Because of stressed living conditions brought on primarily by overcrowding due to overpopulation as well as extensive inter-continental travel, our species is probably more susceptible to pandemics today than ever. We are, due to science and modern medicine, probably better equipped to deal with pandemics today than we were in the past—but less so than is popularly believed.

---

41 Infected rats—the most common carriers of the disease—are believed to have traveled with the traders along established trade routes.

Our best defense against pandemics is to reduce our population to sustainable levels and promote better living conditions for people and livestock everywhere. Virulent viruses may be less likely to originate in affluent areas than impoverished ones, but if a particularly virulent virus surfaced today in Calcutta, India, for example, it could be in Shanghai, New York, London, Moscow, Rome, Beijing, Tokyo, Mexico City, Lima, and every other major metropolitan area within a week, and within a month, it could be virtually everywhere.

It is imperative that we reduce our population to sustainable levels as soon as possible, but it is unlikely that that will happen as long as societies continue to rely on competitive survival strategies for their existence.

4: The Establishment of Artificial Societies

The greater the loyalty of a group toward the group, the greater is the motivation among the members to achieve the goals of the group, and the greater the probability that the group will achieve its goals.

—Rensis Likert

SOCIAL ALLEGIANCE

Until quite recently, our social **allegiances** were limited to family and extended family members, so our social groups were structured around them. And like other social species, we generally regarded *unrelated* members of our species as competitors or even enemies. In other words, we maintained *family*-centric attitudes.

Establishing and maintaining complex, artificial societies, however, required extensive *inter*-familial cooperation and allegiance. We, alone among all species on Earth, have become adept at that, and although it is not generally recognized as such, the establishment of inter-familial allegiance is one of our greatest adaptative accomplishments.

GROWTH AND COMPETITION

Limited availability of food restricted the size of familial, foraging social groups. With the adoption of agricultural, however, increasing availability of food enabled—and increasing occupational demands required—that multifamily social groups grow larger. As they did, competition for resources between them escalated dramatically—frequently leading to conflict. The dynamics of competitive development actually force societies to grow perpetually larger and stronger so they can compete with, and defend themselves from other societies that are doing the same.

Consequently, although we have learned to coexist with non-familial members *within our* societies, we still tend to regard *other* societies as competitors and enemies.

Competition between societies, although natural and understandable, leads inevitably to overpopulation, resource depletion, environmental degradation, and conflict between societies—conditions that impede long-term sustainability.

SOCIOCENTRISM AND CONFLICT

Conflict between civilized societies is very different from conflict between primitive societies. This is partly due to the fact that many more people are involved in civilized conflicts and partly due to the types of weapons used by them.

It is doubtful that many people actually died in primitive confrontations. There is only so much damage that can be done with rocks, clubs, and spears. Generally, when one side exhibited superior strength, the other side assumedly simply acquiesced and retreated.

Death tolls in modern wars, however, can be truly horrendous. There are over one hundred instances in recorded history where more than *ten thousand* people were killed in single battles lasting less than forty-eight hours. There are also more than thirty instances where death tolls exceeded *fifty thousand*, and more than ten instances where they exceeded one *hundred thousand!*[42]

If nuclear weapons were employed in an all-out war between two superpowers today, literally *hundreds of millions* of people could be killed in hours. That almost happened in 1962 during the Cuban missile crisis.

After the United States detonated nuclear bombs over Hiroshima and Nagasaki in 1945, it became clear to the Soviets that whoever was in possession of the most powerful nuclear arsenal would be the dominant nation on Earth and the one that would most likely be able to advance its sociopolitical and economic ideologies. At that time, a sociocentric contest began between the United States (embracing democracy, **capitalism**, and Christianity) and the Soviet Union (embracing secular **socialism**).

By 1962, the United States was in possession of both more missiles and missiles with greater ranges. This disparity of capability was known as the "missile gap." In an attempt to close it, Russian premier Nikita Khrushchev decided to deploy intermediate-range nuclear missiles in Cuba, their close ally. According to Khrushchev, placing missiles in Cuba would "restrain the United States from precipitous military action against Castro's government [in Cuba]" and serve to establish a "balance of power" between the two nations.[43]

Factions within the Kennedy administration, especially his Joint Chiefs of Staff, did not see it that way. They chose to regard the placement of missiles in Cuba as an overt act of aggression and an attempt to establish a powerful communist regime in the Western Hemisphere. In response, Kennedy implemented an embargo on Cuba and issued an ultimatum stating that the Soviets had to disarm the missiles and remove them from Cuba or face severe consequences. This put Khrushchev in a very difficult position. He could not back down and stay in power. A line had been drawn in the sand that neither Kennedy nor Khrushchev could cross without

---

42 http://en.wikipedia.org/wiki/List_of_battles_by_casualties

43 http://ibchayanid.posterous.com/why-did-the-soviet-union-decide-to-place-miss

committing political suicide and, in so doing, possibly relinquishing control of the situation to far more aggressive elements in their governments.

On October 26, 1962, Kennedy received a candid letter from Khrushchev. CIA officials determined that it was probably *not* edited by the Politburo, as it contained uncharacteristically Soviet sentiments regarding the situation:

> Everyone needs peace: both capitalists, if they have not lost their reason, and still more, communists.
>
> War is our enemy and a calamity for all people.
>
> If indeed war should break out, then it would not be in our power to stop it, for such is the logic of war. I have participated in two wars, and I know that war ends only when it has rolled through cities and villages, everywhere sowing death and destruction.
>
> I should like you to agree that one cannot give way to pressures; it is necessary to control them.
>
> If people do not show wisdom, then in the final analysis, they will come to a clash, like blind moles, and then reciprocal extermination will begin.
>
> If you have not lost your self-control, then Mr. President, we and you ought not now to pull on the end of a rope in which you have tied the knot of war, because the more the two of us pull, the tighter the knot will be tied. And a moment may come when that knot will be tied so tight that even he who tied it will not have the strength to untie it. And then it will be necessary to cut that knot.
>
> And what that will mean is not for me to explain to you, because you yourself understand perfectly what terrible forces

our countries possess. Let us not only relax the forces pulling on the end of the rope; let us take means to untie the knot. We are ready for this.

This statement provided everyone involved with a degree of hope that catastrophe could be averted. On the following morning, however, Kennedy received a more assertive message from Khrushchev with demands that he could not accede to. Later that afternoon, the Joint Chiefs recommended that an air strike be launched on Cuba the morning of October 29, followed by a ground invasion seven days later.

Kennedy knew that if the United States attacked Cuba that it would inevitably lead to a nuclear exchange between the United States and the Soviet Union. Astoundingly, both countries were prepared to take the fatal next step. To make matters worse, Kennedy had to make his decision before the missals in Cuba became operational, which, at that time, was just thirty-six hours away.

On the 29th, Kennedy was leaning towards attacking Cuba, but fortunately, Llewellyn "Tommy" Thompson, a former ambassador to Moscow and acquaintance of Khrushchev, suggested they ignore the second communication containing the unacceptable demands and reply to the first one. Regarding that exchange, Secretary of Defense, Robert S. McNamara, stated:

> This is where we come in on what may have been the single most important exchange of the entire crisis on the U.S. side and, given the stakes at that supremely dangerous moment, one of the most important discussions of the entire Cold War. I am quoting from The Kennedy Tapes:
>
> Kennedy: "We're not going to get these weapons out of Cuba, probably, anyway...I mean by negotiation...I don't think there's any doubt he's not going to retreat now that he made that public, Tommy. He's not going to take them out of Cuba."

Thompson: "I don't agree, Mr. President. I think there's still a chance we can get this line going."

Kennedy: "He'll back down?"

Thompson: "The important thing for Khrushchev, it seems to me, is to be able to say 'I saved Cuba; I stopped an invasion,' and he can get away with this, if he wants to, and he's had a go at this Turkey thing, and that we'll discuss later."

Kennedy: "Alright."[44]

Kennedy followed Thompson's advice and responded to Khrushchev's first letter, offering an assurance that he would not invade Cuba (a demand made in the first correspondence). He also eventually agreed to remove US Jupiter missiles from Turkey (a demand made in the second correspondence)—but six months later. This allowed Kennedy to meet the Soviet demands without appearing overly compliant. The missiles were then dismantled and removed from Cuba, averting, at the last minute, nuclear war.

It must have taken a great deal of courage for Kennedy to delay the air strike. In so doing, he gave the Soviet Union first-strike capability. It was a decision that his Joint Chiefs of Staff were firmly opposed to.

In the final analysis, however, it wouldn't have mattered who had struck first, because both the United States and the Soviet Union would have been destroyed. The only rational option was to avoid war, so the decision Kennedy made was the only one worthy of consideration.

We have been taught to believe that the Soviet deployment of missiles in Cuba was an act of aggression against the United States, and that we were totally justified in demanding, even at the risk of starting a nuclear war, that they be removed. This perspective is understandable; however, it is important to remember that, at that time, we had ballistic missiles deployed in Great Brittan and Turkey that could reach every major city in

---

44 http://www.armscontrol.org/act/2002_11/cubanmissile

the Soviet Union. Additionally, between 1961 and 1963, the US government had initiated *six* assassination attempts on Castro.[45] Consequently, a very strong case can be made that Khrushchev's stated intention to protect Castro's government [in Cuba] and to establish a "balance of power" between the United States and the Soviet Union was completely justified.

It is clear that both Kennedy and Khrushchev defied powerful elements within their governments to avoid war, and for that, we should be eternally grateful to them. It is worth pondering how events would have transpired if George W. Bush, for example, had been president of the United States at that time or Joseph Stalin had been general secretary of the Soviet Union. In either case, we probably wouldn't be here now.

CONQUEST

Humans have always fought, but contrary to popular belief, there is no archaeological evidence to suggest that primitive people ever fought wars. Paradoxically, warfare seems to be a manifestation of civilization. We do not know how soon after the adoption of agriculture warfare began, but we do know that the inhabitants of Jericho, Israel were building large defensive walls around their settlement by about 11,000 BP, so it is safe to assume that within a thousand years of its adoption, people were engaging in protracted battles.

Because societies utilize competitive developmental strategies, they need to perpetually gain possession of more land and more resources to support them. The only way they can accomplish that is to take it from others by force. We know that this type of behavior is wrong, but we can usually justify it by villainizing our enemies (competitors) and creating gods who favor us and our causes.

---

45 http://www.globalsecurity.org/intell/ops/castro.htm

Once again, we find evidence of this in the Tanakh. There, when instructing the Israelites how to deal with their enemies (competitors), God allegedly commanded them to:

> ... doom them to destruction: grant them no terms and give them no quarter (Deuteronomy 7:2).

> You shall destroy all the people that the Lord your God delivers to you, showing them no pity (Deuteronomy 7:16).

At Jericho:

> The people rushed into the city, every man straight in front of him, and they captured the city [Jericho]. They exterminated everything in the city with the sword: man and woman, young and old, ox and sheep and ass (Joshua 6:20–21).

And at Ai:

> When Israel had killed all the inhabitants of Ai who had pursued them into the wilderness, and all of them, to the last man had fallen by the sword, all the Israelites turned back to Ai and put it to the sword. The total of those who fell that day, men and women, the entire population of Ai, came to twelve thousand (Joshua 8: 24–25).

A rational argument can be made that fighting to defend oneself is always justified and therefore always moral. Conversely, an equally strong argument can be made that fighting offensively is never justified and therefore always immoral. Many societies (including the United States) owe their existence to offensive conquests of other societies, so it may seem hypocritical for the beneficiary of a conquering nation to criticize the strategy now. However, only by recognizing previous injustices, can we avoid perpetuating them in the future.

The international validation of conquest originated with a Roman law called *terra nullius*. It maintained that unfarmed land was not legally owned by anyone and was therefore subject to seizure. Using that guise, European nations stole most of North America, South America, Africa, and Australia from its indigenous inhabitants. Codifying the theft of that land exemplifies the extreme limits of European sociocentric attitudes and beliefs.

Today, most nations admonish the practice of invasion and conquest, because they do recognize it as immoral behavior. After all, it is difficult to justify a practice that can kill millions of innocent people. Nevertheless, it still happens. A case in point was the 2003 invasion of Iraq by the United States (see Chapter 2: Becoming Human).

In the United States, we regard ourselves as the primary defenders of freedom and human rights in the world today, and yet we invaded and conquered a sovereign nation that posed no immediate risk to us or our allies. This type of irresponsible and immoral behavior will inevitably continue as long as societies maintain extreme sociocentric attitudes and employ highly competitive survival strategies. Once again, we are faced with having to modify behavior that was appropriate in natural states of existence that is not—or is no longer—appropriate in our current artificial state of existence.

5: Government

Nearly all men can stand adversity, but if you want to test a man's character, give him power.

—Abraham Lincoln

RESPONSIBLE LEADERSHIP

Primitive foraging societies were egalitarian and didn't need governments. With the adoption of agriculture and sedentary existence, however, societies quickly became far too large and complex to manage without them. They were faced with having to build roads, granaries, defensive walls, dams, irrigation ditches, sanitation systems, and other projects that were municipal in scope. The larger and more complex societies become, the more comprehensive their governments have to be.

Within artificial societies, populations naturally fragment into various ethnic, class, political, religious, and other special interest groups that vie for recognition. Governments are also needed to ensure that equitable conditions prevail among them.

Throughout human history, people have struggled to find ideal, or at least acceptable, forms of governments. At one end of the spectrum are autocracies that remove all policy-making powers from citizens, and at the other end are democracies, where citizens maintain responsibility for making decisions.

Theoretically, democracies should be the most equitable forms of governments. But they are a long way away from being perfect. They require a level of public awareness and involvement that is generally lacking in most societies. Regarding those shortcomings, Winston Churchill once noted, "The best argument against democracy is a five-minute conversation with the average voter."

Most Americans believe the United States is a democracy, but that is not true. We are actually a republic (which is as close to a democracy as a large, artificial society can practically be). In republics, the public is not directly involved in decision making; they elect representatives to make decisions for them.

Regardless of the type of government, it must establish a body of responsible laws that everyone adheres to. In the United States, that body of laws is the US Constitution. It has survived longer than any other body of laws and it is frequently used as a model by other countries to establish their bodies of laws, so it will be used as an example here.

THE UNITED STATES CONSTITUTION

It is a little known fact, but the US Constitution of 1787 was not our nation's first body of laws. Preceding it was the Articles of Confederation, drafted and approved by members of the second Continental Congress in 1777 and ratified in 1781. It was a total failure. It did not even recognize the United States as a sovereign nation. In Article III, it stated:

> The said States hereby severally enter into a firm league of friendship with each other, for their common defense, the security of their liberties, and their mutual and general welfare, binding themselves to assist each other, against all force offered

to, or attacks made upon them, or any of them, on account of religion, sovereignty, trade, or any other pretense whatever.

In other words, each state was regarded as a separate nation—but one that was committed to cooperating with the other nation-states. The federal government was given so little power in the Articles of Confederation that, by 1787, nearly every member of Congress agreed that it had to be amended. Unfortunately, Article XIII of the Articles prohibited changes without ratification by every state:

> And the Articles of this confederation shall be inviolably observed by every State, and the union shall be perpetual; nor shall any alteration at any time hereafter be made in any of them; unless such alteration be agreed to in a congress of the united States, and be afterwards confirmed by the legislatures of every State.

Due to the difficulties this stipulation presented, the members of Congress decided to draft a completely new document. Technically, this was an act of treason, but since it had nearly unanimous support, it never became an issue. In any event, the US Constitution was drafted over a period of several months—in closed sessions—and was approved on September 17, 1787. It is truly a remarkable document, and the fact that it has lasted for more than two hundred years is a testament to its authors' wisdom and integrity, but it is far from being perfect, and the founding fathers knew it.

PREAMBLE

Gouverneur Morris, from Pennsylvania, is generally acknowledged as the author of the Preamble of the US Constitution. It defined the responsibilities of a government about as well as any single paragraph can:

> We the People of the United States, in Order to form a more
> perfect Union, establish Justice, insure domestic Tranquility,
> provide for the common defence,[46] promote the general
> Welfare, and secure the Blessings of Liberty to ourselves and
> our Posterity, do ordain and establish this Constitution for the
> United States of America.

Unfortunately, there was quite a bit of disagreement as to just who *ourselves* and *our posterity* were. Representatives from the southern states did not want African Americans to be included in that category, while representatives from the northern states did. In fact, Thomas Jefferson initially included a passage in the Declaration of Independence that abolished slavery. But it was removed, because he knew that representatives from the southern states would not sign it if it remained. The same thing happened when drafting the Constitution. It originally included a provision granting civil rights to African Americans, but it was also removed to make it more acceptable to the southern states.

This presented a dilemma to representatives from the southern states. A high percentage of their populations were composed of African American slaves. If they didn't count them as citizens, then they would be under-represented in the new federal government. However, if they did count them, they would then have to recognize their civil rights. That problem was solved—very cleverly, but not very equitably or honorably—with what came to be known as the Three-Fifths Compromise. That issue was so important to the passage of the Constitution that it was actually specifically addressed in Article 1 (Section 2, Paragraph 3). It states:

> Representatives and direct Taxes shall be apportioned among
> the several States which may be included within this Union,
> according to their respective Numbers, which shall be
> determined by adding to the whole Number of free Persons,

---

46 Defence was the accepted spelling for defense at that time.

including those bound to Service for a Term of Years, and
excluding Indians not taxed, three fifths of all other Persons.

In other words, each African American was initially regarded as *three-fifths* of a citizen by the US Constitution. Clearly, the US government was not powerful enough at that time to "secure the Blessings of Liberty" for everyone, and sadly, it still isn't.

So, contrary to popular belief, our founding fathers did not quite establish either a democracy or a republic. It was more of a democratic oligarchy. Nevertheless, the drafting and ratification of the US Constitution was a seminal event—not only to our nation, but many others as well.

Beyond what the Constitution accomplished, its authors wisely recognized that it was not perfect and would need to be amended periodically. Consequently, they included Article V, which states:

The Congress, whenever two thirds of both Houses shall deem
it necessary, shall propose Amendments to this Constitution....

Over the next 205 years, twenty-seven amendments were added, the most significant of which are the following:

- Amendments 1–10: The Bill of Rights (December 15, 1791)

- Amendment 13: Slavery Abolished (December 6, 1865)

- Amendment 14: Citizenship Rights (July 9, 1868)

- Amendment 15: Race No Bar to Vote (February 3, 1870)

- Amendment 19: Women's Suffrage (August 18, 1920)

These amendments served to address some of the compromises and omissions that were made in the original document—the most contentious of which have always revolved around the allocation of responsibilities of the federal government as they affect states' rights to determine human rights. The bloodiest war the United States ever fought was a war between the *un*united states in an attempt to resolve those issues. It almost succeeded, and quite possibly would have, if Lincoln had not been assassinated and replaced by Vice President Andrew Johnson. Unfortunately, Johnson was a southern sympathizer and quite literally squandered the opportunity created by Lincoln and the Civil War to unite the country under more equitable laws.

LEADERSHIP

Artificial societies cannot function without governments, governments cannot function without leaders, and leaders cannot manage societies without power.

The voluntary transfer of power from individuals to leaders is the ultimate manifestation of public trust. The effectiveness of this strategy is dependent, to a large degree, on society's ability to choose dependable leaders. If they choose wisely, they will generally prosper. If they do not, they will inevitably suffer.

In primitive societies, the most respected male and/or female members generally *assumed* leadership roles. They did not seek those positions; they were regarded as obligations. Leadership roles in artificial societies are very different. They have evolved into full-time positions that offer leaders enormous personal benefits. Consequently, they tend to attract self-serving or egocentric individuals who not only seek them, they frequently resort to deception and/or coercion to attain them.

The acquisition of power by individuals who do not deserve it is a chronic problem intrinsic to artificial existence and one that requires constant public vigilance to control.

TOO MUCH POWER

Leaders are necessarily given a great deal of power so that they can manage societies. Unfortunately, their natures, in conjunction with the demands of their positions, sometimes encourages them to acquire more power than is allocated to them. Their quest for increased power is far more likely to be successful during real or perceived national emergencies.

There may be times when it is appropriate to grant leaders additional power, but there are enormous risks involved. Two recent and graphic examples include the passage of the USA Patriot Act under George W. Bush in 2001 (see Chapter 2: Becoming Human) and the passage of the Gulf of Tonkin Resolution under Lyndon B. Johnson in 1964.

In 1964, the United States was engaged in the Cold War with the Soviet Union and was committed to stopping the spread of communism. In August of that year, two US destroyers, the USS *Maddox* and the USS *C. Turner Joy* were operating in the Gulf of Tonkin southeast of Vietnam. At 8:00 p.m. on August 4, they received radio reports that gave the "impression" that North Vietnamese patrol boats might be planning to attack them. Air reconnaissance was provided for the destroyers by the carrier USS *Ticonderoga*, but its pilots were not able to locate any enemy craft.

However, at about 10:00 p.m., sonar operators on the *Maddox* reported approaching torpedoes. The destroyers initiated evasive maneuvers and fired upon the locations where they thought the North Vietnamese patrol boats might have been. Soon after that, US naval officers reported sinking two, or possibly three, North Vietnamese boats—even though none had ever been sighted. After aerial reconnaissance the following morning failed to find any flotsam from these boats, however, Captain Herrick admitted that the blips on the radar screen were probably "freak weather effects" and that the report of torpedoes might have come from "overeager" radar operators.[47]

President Lyndon Johnson was provided with all of the reports regarding the alleged attack, but chose to ignore those that did not support it. Instead, he decided to launch "retaliatory" air strikes on North Vietnamese torpedo-boat bases. That evening, he announced (lied) to the American public that US naval forces had been attacked, and that he was requesting Congressional approval of a resolution:

---

47 http://www.history.com/this-day-in-history/reported-north-vietnamese-pt-boat-attacks-result-in-retaliation-strikes

expressing the unity and determination of the United States in supporting freedom and in protecting peace in Southeast Asia.

On August 10, 1964, after a very brief meeting, Congress unanimously voted to pass the Gulf of Tonkin Resolution. This resolution gave Johnson the power to engage the North Vietnamese without congressional oversight—a power that he arguably exercised imprudently. By 1968, he had committed 536,000 troops to fight in Vietnam. Tragically, more than fifty-eight thousand of them, and as many as two million Vietnamese troops were killed in what turned out to be a completely pointless war fought under false pretenses.

It is entirely possible that both Johnson and Bush believed they were acting in their country's the best interests when they decided to invade Viet Nam and Iraq. However, a strong case can be made that they did not have the right to make those decisions—even if they had the power to do so. More to the point, they should never have been given that much power.

SPECIAL INTERESTS

BUSINESS

In the United States, we get to elect governmental representatives, but seldom do those representatives represent us. Their campaigns are typically financed directly or indirectly by large corporations, so, regardless of their political affiliations, representatives owe greater allegiance to business interests than they do to us. Technically, this means that the United States is now more of a *corporatocracy* than a republic.

Governments obviously need to provide environments that are conducive to business, but allowing business to direct governmental policy through campaign manipulation is a recipe for social and environmental disaster. Businesses are concerned with profit—not the public, not their societies, and not the environment.

Many government officials are opposed to corporate intervention in government, but most of them are beholden to business interests in one way or the other. Consequently, they cannot afford to initiate or even support reforms that would limit their involvement.

The collusive relationship between business and government has been in existence for a long time. Boies Penrose, a Republican senator from Pennsylvania described how it works to a group of his supporters in 1896:

> I believe in the division of labor. You send us to Congress; we pass laws under which you make money…and out of your profits, you further contribute to our campaign funds to send us back again to pass more laws to enable you to make more money. (Nader 2004, 25)

Another way that corporations influence governmental policy is to have *their* employees appointed to influential positions in governments (see Chapter 3: The Adoption of Agriculture). This approach clearly establishes conflicts of interest, but it is tolerated, because those in power are those who benefit from it. A graphic example of this type of collusion recently occurred between former Vice President Dick Chaney and the mega corporation Halliburton.

Unless otherwise noted, the following information was obtained from the Halliburton Watch website,[48] which was compiled by Agnes Christeler:

1989

- Dick Cheney became secretary of defense under George H. W. Bush.

1992

- Under Cheney's direction, a subsidiary of Halliburton, Brown & Root, was paid $9 million by the Pentagon to produce a

---

48 http://www.halliburtonwatch.org/about_hal/chronology.html

report outlining how private companies (like itself) could provide logistical support for American troops abroad.

- Soon afterward, the Pentagon awarded Brown & Root a five-year contract to provide logistics for the US Army Corp of Engineers—worth approximately $2.2 million.

1995

- With no previous business experience, Cheney was given the CEO position at Halliburton Co., one of the world's largest oil consortiums.

- Under Cheney's leadership, Halliburton moved up from seventy-third to eighteenth on the Pentagon's list of top contractors.

- The US government awarded Halliburton $2.3 billion in contracts (up from $1.2 billion the previous year).

- Revenue from Halliburton's overseas operations rose from 51 percent to 68 percent of its total revenue since Cheney became CEO.

- Halliburton received $1.5 billion in assistance from government-sponsored agencies such as OPIC (Overseas Private Investment Corporation) and the Export-Import Bank (up from $100 million for the five years prior to Cheney's arrival).

1999

- The US military awarded Halliburton's Kellogg, Brown & Root with a contract worth $180 million a year to supply US forces in the Balkans with logistical support.

2000

- Cheney became vice president under George W. Bush.

- Halliburton gave Cheney a retirement package worth more than $33.7 million.

- Halliburton became the world's largest diversified energy service, with $15 billion in revenues annually, one hundred thousand employees and seven thousand customers in over 120 countries.

2001

- The US Navy awarded Kellogg, Brown & Root an exclusive $300 million contract to supply logistics to the Navy.

- Kellogg, Brown & Root was paid $2 million to reinforce the US embassy in Tashkent, Uzbekistan, under contract with the State Department.

- The Pentagon awarded Kellogg, Brown & Root a ten-year cost-plus-award-fee contract[49] to provide support services to the Army. The contract allowed the federal government an open-ended mandate and budget to send Kellogg, Brown & Root anywhere in the world to run humanitarian or military operations for profit.

2002

- The US government awarded Kellogg, Brown & Root contracts totaling more than $1.3 billion.

2003

- Cheney supported the United States invasion of Iraq, even though there was no justifiable reason for doing so.

---

49 http://www.corpwatch.org/article.php?id=2471

- The US Army Corps of Engineers awarded a no-bid contract, with a cost ceiling of $7 billion, to Kellogg, Brown & Root to extinguish oil well fires in Iraq.

- On September 14, while being interviewed on NBC's *Meet the Press*, Cheney was asked about his connections with Halliburton. He responded:

And since I left Halliburton to become George Bush's vice president, I've severed all my ties with the company [Halliburton], gotten rid of all my financial interest. I have no financial interest in Halliburton of any kind and haven't had, now, for over three years.

But that wasn't true. At that time, Cheney was still receiving a deferred salary of over $150,000 per year from Halliburton and retained more than four hundred thousand shares of unexercised stock options.

Remarkably, to this day, no one knows exactly why *we* invaded Iraq. Richard Clarke offered five reasons in *Against All Enemies: Inside America's War on Terror* (2004) attributed to three senior White House advisors—Dick Cheney, Donald Rumsfeld, and Paul Wolfowitz—and to President Bush:

- To clean up the mess left by the first Bush administration when, in 1991, it let Saddam Hussein consolidate power and slaughter opponents after the first Iraqi war;

- To improve Israel's strategic position by eliminating a large, hostile military;

- To create an Arab democracy that could serve as a model to other friendly Arab states now threatened with internal dissent, notably Egypt and Saudi Arabia;

- To permit the withdrawal of US forces from Saudi Arabia (after twelve years), where they were stationed to counter the Iraqi military and were a source of anti-Americanism threatening to the regime; and

- To create another friendly source of oil for the US market and reduce dependency upon oil from Saudi Arabia, which might suffer overthrow someday.

Bush, Cheney, Rumsfeld, and Wolfowitz were all looking for an excuse to invade Iraq, but why? We may never know the answer to that question. But we do know that Dick Cheney received large sums of money from a company that benefited enormously from government contracts granted to it during Cheney's terms of "public" service. Coincidence?

Business would like us to believe that the world runs on commerce, and although civilization does rely on commerce, the rest of the world actually runs in spite of it. Business is concerned with short-term profit, not the well-being of societies, Earth's biota, or the environment.

RELIGION

In the United States, we have been reasonably successful in insulating government from religion. Contrary to popular belief, however, there is no provision in the US Constitution that specifically addresses it. In a letter[50] written to the Danbury Baptist Association in 1802, Thomas Jefferson mentioned the need for a "wall of separation between church and state," but the closest the Constitution comes to addressing it appears in the First Amendment, and it only states, "Congress shall make no law respecting an establishment of religion...."

Governments need to ensure religious freedom, but it is important to realize that religions are self-serving entities. They feign piety, but

---

50 http://www.usconstitution.net/jeffwall.html

aggressively pursue power, influence and revenue in much the same way that businesses do. As such, they should never allowed to influence governmental policies.

Alarmingly, beginning in 1990, Jefferson's wall of separation was breached. At that time, the Christian Coalition, a Christian organization founded by Pat Robertson, began to infiltrate the Republican Party. Robertson laid out a strategy for taking over the party in his book *The Millennium*. In it, he stated:

> With the apathy that exists today, a well-organized minority can influence the selection of candidates to an astonishing degree.[51]

Robertson was right. A righteous minority can easily overpower an apathetic or complacent majority. In a very real sense, the Christian Coalition sought, and found a way, to circumvent the will of the majority by deceiving and/or indoctrinating them to vote certain ways. According to the Christian Coalition website, their:

> … hallmark work lies in voter education. Each election year, Christian Coalition distributes tens of millions of voter guides throughout all fifty states, (up to seventy million in 2000 alone!). These guides help give voters a clear understanding of where candidates stand on important pro-family issues—before they go to the polls on Election Day.[52]

Contrary to its claim, however, its goal is not to educate; it is to indoctrinate. In June 1999, the federal government recognized this and rescinded its tax-exemption. Nevertheless, its impact on government through the Republican Party has been profound. It is quite likely that George W. Bush, for example, would not have been elected or reelected president if he had not received backing from the Christian Coalition. It has transformed

51 http://www.theocracywatch.org/taking_over.htm
52 http://www.cc.org/about_us

the Republican Party into what is fundamentally a conservative, Christian political party.

The public needs to recognize that religions are essentially businesses based on irrational dogmas. Governments should consider their needs, but religions should never be allowed to unduly influence governmental policy. The results will always be extremely biased.

POLITICAL PARTISANSHIP

In most societies, ideologically "conservative" and "liberal" political factions or parties vie for control of governments. Each party believes that its ideology is "right" and the others' is "wrong." Those beliefs are absurd. The primary difference between them is whom they represent. Presently, in the United States, the Conservative (Republican) Party generally represents big business and the upper classes, while the Liberal (Democratic) Party generally represents laborers, minorities, and the lower classes. This is a simplistic explanation of party politics, but it serves well to illustrate the fact that neither party is committed to equitable representation, and that neither party is inherently "right" or "wrong."

Political parties also believe that their ideologies are diametrically opposed. Those beliefs are also absurd. Both parties respond to issues from within the same narrow parameters of cultural indoctrination. They may be diametrically opposed within those narrow bands, but that is akin to two individuals driving side by side on an open highway, arguing about which lane is better. One is in the left lane and the other is in the right lane, but they are both headed in the same direction, and they will both arrive at the same destination.

Between 1976 and 1984, in an attempt to provide voters with pertinent information regarding the qualifications of potential candidates, the League of Women Voters sponsored presidential debates. During that time, the league kept the two major parties from manipulating the debates, ensuring that they were open to popular independent candidates.

By 1986, however, the two major parties successfully gained control of the debates and, in 1987, formed a private corporation called the Commission on Presidential Debates (CPD). Since then, the CPD has sponsored all presidential debates and handled all of the debate contracts. The CPD refuses to release the particulars of these contracts, but it is known that large corporations (such as Philip Morris and Anheuser-Busch) are major contributors.

Remarkably, in 1988, under the CPD, Bush and Dukakis campaign strategists drafted a secret debate contract called the "Memorandum of Understanding." It regulated and restricted the debate parameters to the degree that the League of Women Voters claimed it perpetrated "a fraud on the American voter."

The integrity of the presidential debates, unfortunately, has gone downhill since then. The two co-chairs who control the CPD—Frank Fahrenkopf and Paul Kirk—are registered lobbyists for multinational corporations. Regarding their capacities to influence the outcomes of elections by manipulating the debates, Fahrenkopf responded, "We're not going to apologize for trying to influence political elections."

Currently, presidential debates are, for all practical purposes, partisan and far less effective than they could be in providing voters with pertinent information regarding candidates. Since 1987, the CPD debate protocols have disallowed challenging questions, assertive moderators, follow-up questions, candidate-to-candidate questioning, and rebuttals. The debates have basically become a sham in which the two opponents have previously agreed not to address contentious issues. In regard to them, Walter Cronkite, respected anchorman for CBS Evening News for nineteen years, commented that CPD-sponsored presidential debates were an "unconscionable fraud."[53]

Of additional concern is that our rigid two-party system excludes potentially worthy candidates—not only from ballot access but also from

---

53 http://www.projectcensored.org/top-stories/articles/20-secret-control-of-the-
   presidential-debates/

debates. During the 2000 presidential debates, for example, Ralph Nader, arguably one of the most qualified, capable, and conscientious candidates we have had in recent years, was not only not allowed to participate in the debates, he was forbidden from even attending them!

When Nader showed up at the first debate with a valid ticket (which had been donated to him by a fan), he was met by the CPD's security consultant and *state police* and forced to leave under threat of arrest![54]

If the public had had the opportunity to witness an unregulated, three-way debate between Bush, Gore, and Nader, Nader would almost certainly have demonstrated a greater understanding of the most pressing political, economic, social, and environmental issues than either of the other candidates.

Furthermore, if Nader had been elected president, he would have been free to lead more objectively than either Bush or Gore because of his Independent affiliation. Imagine having a president whose primary allegiance was to the public, not to political parties or corporations. If Nader had been elected President, the United States would probably be in much better shape—politically, economically, socially, and environmentally—than it is today.

Artificial societies cannot function without governments, and governments cannot function without leaders, but we currently have no way to consistently select reliable leaders. This is a problem that will have to be resolved before we can attain, or even seriously pursue, sustainability (see Chapter 19: Reform Government).

---

54 http://www.gp.org/press/pr_04_16_02.html

6: Commerce

He who is not contented with what he has would not be contented with what he would like to have.

—Socrates

INCEPTION OF COMMERCE

People no doubt bartered products and services before the adoption of agriculture, but true commerce began soon after its inception.

In order for agriculture to function as a primary subsistence strategy, farmers need to plant, harvest, and store far more crops than they actually need in any given year. Substantial portions of annual crops can be lost to insect infestations, droughts, disease, etc. Consequently, agriculturalists have to overproduce crops when possible, and store them for use in the event of future crop failures.

Utilizing that strategy inevitably leads to the accumulation of excess crops. Not surprisingly, farmers quickly learned that excess crops could be bartered for other products or services. At that time, crops became the first true commodities, and their trading marked the inception of true commerce.

Commerce is a dynamic activity that spurs innovation and development, but we need to realize that its motive is to generate profit—not to benefit societies or advance civilization.

COMPETITION FOR WEALTH

Once the concept of commerce was realized, people compulsively began to accumulate wealth: first probably as stored crops, then as land, and eventually as various forms of currencies.

This compulsion is almost certainly an extension of our age-old instinct as foragers to hoard as much food as possible to survive winter seasons. The primary difference being that foragers could never hoard more food than they could preserve and consume in a single winter, while competitive individuals in agricultural societies can accumulate more wealth than—if converted to food—could be consumed in many lifetimes.

The acquisition of wealth also frequently leads to severe social **inequity**. Social inequity probably began soon after the adoption of agriculture twelve thousand years ago. Certainly, it was an issue by 3,300 years ago, because it was addressed in Genesis. At that time, Joseph allegedly purchased all of the surplus crops in Egypt when they were available, then sold them back to the Egyptians at enormous profit over a seven-year period when there were crop failures (Genesis 41-47).

It is unlikely that this event actually occurred—at least as it is related in Genesis—but it demonstrates that people were not only regarding crop surpluses as commodities more than three thousand years ago, they were regarding them as commodities in futures markets!

Two important aspects of artificial development were addressed in Genesis: first, agriculture has the capacity to provide survival security for a large number of people over an extended period of time; second, free market commerce can enable a very few individuals to profit enormously at the expense of a great many individuals. This is the nature of free market enterprise. It is motivated by profit—not the general welfare of societies.

In both natural and artificial states of existence, competition is necessary. However, unrestrained competition for wealth and/or power leads inevitably to social inequities that inhibit social solidarity and the positive advancement of civilization.

UPPER-CLASS CENTRISM

Social inequity stems from class centrism—class centrism occurs as a result of occupational diversification and specialization—and occupational diversification and specialization are inevitable consequences of artificial development.

In primitive societies, roles were determined primarily by age and gender. With the adoption of agriculture and sedentary existence, however, roles diversified—forcing individuals to adopt specialized occupations. People became farmers, herders, masons, carpenters, weavers, potters, etc. As time passed and societies grew even larger and more complex, diversification continued to increase—forcing people to become administrators, lawyers, doctors, police, soldiers, etc. Increasing occupational diversification and specialization is intrinsic to civilized existence and it will undoubtedly continue until civilization collapses.

Specialized occupations require vastly different levels of commitment and skill to perform them. Individuals who practice occupations at similar levels naturally gravitate together. This tendency is inevitable, but it leads to social stratification and upper-class centrism.

Social stratification is not necessarily negative to societies—as long as it remains reasonably equitable. Unfortunately, it seldom does. In the United States, for example:

- 35 percent of the wealth is held by 1 percent of the population,

- 50 percent of the wealth is held by 19 percent of the population, while only

- 15 percent of the wealth is held by 85 percent of the population[55]

---

55 http://sociology.ucsc.edu/whorulesamerica/power/wealth.html

The actual distribution of wealth is not as important to the welfare of societies as whether people on the lower end of the scale have enough "wealth" to maintain healthy, happy, productive lives. In the United States, they do—but barely. In much of the rest of the world, however, they do not. Unfortunately, recent studies indicate that this disparity is increasing.

Severe social inequity stems from upper-class centrism and it is extremely harmful to societies. It prevails because individuals in the upper (ruling) classes establish and maintain social paradigms that favor themselves and their progeny. They accomplish that by ensuring that the lower classes remain poorly educated and without equal opportunities for social advancement.

At the very least, societies suffer because a great deal of the potential technological, intellectual, and social contributions that members from the lower classes could make if given equal opportunity are never realized. And at the very worst, societies collapse because when social inequity becomes severe enough, it inevitably leads to social unrest and revolution.

Ironically, the upper-classes in societies strive to establish biased social paradigms solely so that they and their progeny do not have to compete with members from the lower classes to maintain their privileged statuses.

Social stratification may be inevitable in civilized societies, but oppressive social inequity is not. It exists solely because the upper- classes initiate and perpetuate it. This does not mean that governments should try to mandate social equality. It only means that loyalties to societies should supersede loyalties to social classes—and that means discouraging upper-class centrism.

CONSCIENCE OR REGULATION

Before the adoption of agriculture, humans never possessed—or needed to possess—much more than a few personal items. Once they realized the value of surplus crops and began to regard them as commodities, however, that changed in a big way. Almost overnight, the motives for working shifted from subsistence to commercial—a phenomenon unique to sedentary, agro-industrial existence.

There is nothing intrinsically wrong with commerce. In fact, it is essential to the establishment and maintenance of artificial societies. But commerce tends to bring out the worst in people. Most alarmingly, they develop compulsions to maximize profits without regard to the long-term interests of our species, other species, and the environment—a condition that can best be described as *commerce without conscience*. Unrestrained commerce can lead to rapid fiscal growth for the most aggressive and competitive individuals and businesses over the short-term, but it frequently causes chronic problems in societies and to the environment over the long-term.

Even so, the public generally supports, or at least condones, unrestrained commerce, because we have been indoctrinated to believe that our society's existence is dependent upon it. We *are* dependent on commerce, but our long-term existence is dependent upon maintaining healthy societies and environments. Consequently, we cannot buy into the claim that irresponsible commerce is acceptable. It must be practiced with increased conscience, or it must be regulated. This will require greater public awareness, less tolerance of deception and indoctrination, and campaign reform to eliminate—or at least lessen—business influence in government (see Chapter 19: Reform Government).

7: Religion

Religion is regarded by the common people as true, by the wise as false, and by the rulers as useful.

—Seneca (Roman philosopher, first century CE)

Religions have enormous impacts on civilization. We tend to take their existence for granted, but their success is inexplicable, because they provide no products and no verifiable services.

In order for religions to establish and maintain themselves, they must successfully indoctrinate people with *their* religious dogma. They accomplish that through fear. In the case of the two most successfully promoted religions, Christianity and Islam, fear is established by advancing a truly terrifying entity who attempts to lead us astray (the devil), and a truly horrific place of everlasting torment where we go when we die if we allow ourselves to be lead astray (hell). Specific religions must convince us that the only thing that stands between us and everlasting torment is them.

Most religious dogma is extremely improbable. Consequently, successful religious indoctrination must begin with young children who are naive and especially susceptible to it. Religions claim that they exist to serve us, but evidence suggests that we are coerced into serving, or at least supporting, them.

Currently, more than 85 percent of the world's population contributes to the support of one religion or another. Christianity accounts for 32 percent of that total and Islam, 22 percent of it. The other 31 percent is divided between many smaller religions.[56] The fact that so many people are willing to support religions today is not an indication that they perform valued functions in societies; it is an indication that they have been extremely well promoted.

Remarkably there are no laws, or even cultural mores, restricting the dissemination of irrational dogmas by religions to solicit support for themselves. This is truly remarkable, because religious dogmas are responsible for much of the social unrest and conflict that exists in the world today.

In light of these considerations, while exploring ways to increase our awareness and modify our behavior, we need to objectively examine the nature of faith and the roles of religions in civilization. There are many thousands of different religions and denominations. However, because the Abrahamic religions (Judaism, Christianity, and Islam) are currently the most influential and/or dominant religions, they alone will be evaluated here.

ORIGINS

No one knows what entities, if any, were deified by primitive foragers or even the earliest agriculturalists. All we know for certain is that in the Middle East, in the fourth millennium BCE (when people first began to record information about their beliefs), they were worshiping the sun.

We don't know why people began to deify and worship entities like the sun, but logically, three conditions had to be met before they would. People had to:

- recognize that certain entities were powerful,

- recognize their dependence on them, and

- believe that they were alive or animate

---

56 http://www.religioustolerance.org/worldrel.htm

Humankind has probably always recognized the power and importance of the sun. After all, its presence brings light and warmth, and its absence leaves darkness and cold. It is also easy to imagine why our distant ancestors believed that the sun was alive. After all, it appears to rise above the eastern horizon, travel across the daytime sky, and set below the western horizon. Additionally, they undoubtedly observed vagaries in the sun's behavior. The sun doesn't always rise or set in the same locations or produce the same amount of heat. How could an entity move and behave unless it was alive?

When people realized that their survival depended upon a moody entity that wandered around the sky and disappeared for fairly long periods of time, they understandably became concerned. What if the sun *decided* to leave and not come back? Since people had no control over the sun, they conceivably attempted to placate it with prayers and offerings, in so doing, they created a god.

When we consider the paucity of information that was available to people at that time, their conclusions regarding the sun were not illogical. Nevertheless, they were wrong. The most important consideration regarding early religious beliefs is that the entities they worshiped were not deities and did not hear or answer their prayers, but people were convinced that they were, and did, for many thousands of years.

PROPHETS

Once the sun was accepted as a deity, using the same type of logic in the absence of sufficient accurate information, people began to create deities from other celestial entities that moved across the sky such as the moon, other planets, and constellations. They also began to deify forces on Earth such as lightning, thunder, rain, wind, etc.

Soon after the concept of deities was established, individuals began to surface who claimed they could commune with gods. These prophets convinced ruling members of their societies (and possibly even themselves) that they could solicit favor with gods—helping to ward off calamity and ensure prosperity. Remarkably, they succeeded in creating prominent positions for themselves in their societies by providing totally imaginary services.

Claiming communion with deities has always been a risky proposition. Prophets who happened to live in prosperous times assumedly enjoyed social and economic prosperity. However, those who were unfortunate enough to live in calamitous times were frequently executed as charlatans. Nevertheless, the potential rewards for prophets were sufficient to ensure there were always plenty of claimants competing for recognition within their societies. And as time passed, prophets learned how to offset the risks associated with calamities. They invented and promoted a single all-powerful, invisible, intangible, vengeful, male deity: God.

The promotion of God was truly brilliant. Once "his" existence was accepted, prophets were able to absolve themselves from all culpability. They accomplished that by insisting that God wanted them to adhere to laws that could not possibly always be adhered to. Then, when catastrophes occurred, prophets blamed their disobedient, sinful societies for angering God. This strategy worked so well that it is still in use today.

GOD

There are a number of problems associated with beliefs in invisible, intangible deities. The first is that because they cannot be seen or touched, their existence must be based solely on faith, not actual observations. The existence of gods, therefore, cannot be conveyed as accurate information through education. Their alleged existences must be promoted as dogmas through indoctrination. Consequently, beliefs in gods are inherently irrational beliefs.

IMMORTALITY

As far as is known, Judaism was the first major religion[57] to embrace mono-theism, and if you have read the Tanakh or Old Testament, you know that it got off to a rocky start. It was a novel idea, but comprehensive support for monotheism did not occur until the concepts of immortality, heaven, hell, and the devil were introduced.

The origins of those concepts are murky, but most religious scholars attribute them to **Zoroastrianism**, a religion that arose in Persia (Iran) during the sixth century BCE.[58]

Jews claim they have always recognized the immortality of human souls. But the concept of resurrection was not addressed in the Tanakh until after Jews had been exposed to Zoroastrianism during their exile in Babylon in the early sixth century BCE. Consequently, it is reasonable to assume that the concept was incorporated into Judaism at that time—rather than intrinsic to it (Daniel 12:1–3).

Even so, Jews do not recognize heaven and hell as places where good and evil people go when they die. Those concepts were initially—or at least most successfully—promoted by Paul through Christianity in the New Testament in the first century CE,[59] and then by Muhammad with the introduction of Islam in the seventh century CE.

In Judaism, hell was simply a place below ground where people went after they died—a logical perception, because most people were buried there. However, in Christianity, hell is perceived as a place of everlasting torment reserved for those who do not accept Jesus as their savior, and in Islam, for those who do not embrace Allah and the teachings of Muhammad.

---

57 Zoroastrianism predates Judaism, but it is not regarded as a major religion.

58 Zoroastrianism is still practiced today.

59 CE (Common Era) correlates to the Gregorian calendar designation CE (anno Domini—Latin for "in the year of our Lord").

The earliest reference to Satan is in the Tanakh. There, in Job 1:6, ha-Satan is described as a servant of God whose job it is to test man's devotion to him. In Judaism, Christianity, and Islam, Satan can technically be anyone who questions or challenges their dogmas. But in Christianity and Islam, Satan is perceived as a truly fearsome entity.

Christianity and Islam both promise the attainment of paradise (or heaven) to their adherents when they die. But the requirements for getting there are very different. In Christianity, Paul promoted the concept that paradise could only be attained by those who were baptized and accepted Jesus as their savior. Fulfilling these simple requirements was a small price to pay for possible eternal salvation. Many people at that time were horribly oppressed, so the prospect of attaining some reward for their earthly trials in an afterlife must have been appealing to them. Additionally, converts were not required to follow strict laws—such as Jews were—in order find favor with God. They could, in fact, lead despicable lives and still go to heaven. That covenant of Paul's was, and is, considered an outrageous travesty by Jews and Muslims, who insist that God rewards only those who lead exemplary lives as defined in their scriptures.

Christianity and Islam both advance their causes by offering the rewards of everlasting salvation in heaven for compliancy and the punishment of everlasting damnation in hell for noncompliancy. Remarkably, they have elicited an enormous amount of support for themselves through the promotion of these concepts—even though neither of them has ever demonstrated that heaven or hell even exist. Many rational individuals claim they do not believe in heaven and hell, but they are not so certain that they are willing to risk the consequences of being wrong. Therefore, many of them—albeit grudgingly—support religions that promote those concepts.

The dissemination of the concept of an afterlife has been enormously successful for Christianity and Islam, but there is a tragic consequence to it that is seldom considered. Many Christians and Muslims believe that their earthly existences are merely burdens that must be endured until they die and go to heaven. Unfortunately, their preoccupation with life after death frequently prevents them from fully appreciating their earthly lives.

RELIGIOUS TEXTS

The Abrahamic religions are based on laws and directives recorded in texts allegedly provided to them directly or indirectly by God. They are:

- The Tanakh (Judaism),

- The Holy Bible (Christianity), and

- The Quran (Islam)

Members of each faith maintain that by adhering to *their* religious texts that they are following God's laws and serving his will. Religious texts can be interpreted literally or allegorically. Fundamentalist practitioners believe that because their texts allegedly contain the actual words of God that they must be interpreted literally. Progressive observers, on the other hand, recognize that events related in their religious texts are frequently not credible and must therefore be interpreted allegorically. An apt analogy to this situation is as follows:

Imagine that an individual witnessed and recorded an event in 1900. In it they described a "great horned owl" with a ten-foot wingspan. Then, one hundred years later, someone used that account to describe the same event again. Is there any possible way, assuming there is no additional information available, that the event can be described more accurately in 2000 than it was in 1900?

The fundamentalist viewpoint is that it cannot. Any change to the original account has to be regarded as a revision and, therefore, a corruption of it. Whereas the progressive viewpoint is that the original account must have been wrong, because great horned owls do not, and never have had, wingspans that exceed four feet. Consequently, they insist that the account must be revised in order to make it more credible.

Fundamentalist versus progressive doctrinal interpretations may seem trivial, but millions of people have fought and died over them in the last two thousand years.

If any religion is in possession of a text containing the actual words/ laws of God as provided by God, then that text would assumedly reveal laws that should be adhered to by everyone. But neither Jews, Christians, nor Muslims are in possession of such a text. The best they can claim is that they are in possession of accurate **facsimiles** of texts provided to them by God, which, of course, they all do.

In order to assess the legitimacy of their claims, the credibility of the contents of their texts has to be evaluated objectively. If the contents prove highly probable and historically accurate, then the texts should be regarded as credible, and the claims regarding their divinity should be regarded as *possible*. Conversely, texts that do not prove highly probable *and* historically accurate, should be regarded as *not* credible, and the claims regarding their divinity should be regarded as *unlikely*.

THE TANAKH (JUDAISM)

The Jewish religious text is the Tanakh. It contains:

- The Torah (Pentateuch, or the Five Books of Moses),

- The Neviim (Prophets), and

- The Ketuvim (Writings).

Jews claim that the Torah was given to Moses by God and recorded by him in the 1300s BCE. The oldest known Torah is in a copy of the Tanakh known as the Leningrad Codex, which was written in 1009 CE. Consequently, 2,300 years separate the alleged original writing of the Torah and the earliest known extant copy of it. To their credit, Jews have demonstrated a tradition of meticulous transcriptions of the Tanakh. However, their claim to be in possession of an accurate facsimile of a text written by Moses more than three thousand years ago is extremely unlikely. Even if they were in possession of such a text, that would not necessarily mean that it was divine. In order to determine its credibility, we need to objectively evaluate its content, specifically the earliest accounts in the Torah.

CREATION

According to Genesis 1–2, God created the universe in the following order:

- Day 1: heaven, Earth, and light (light and darkness were separated and given the designations: day and night)

- Day 2: sky

- Day 3: land and vegetation

- Day 4: "lights" in the sky (the sun and the moon)

- Day 5: marine animals and birds

- Day 6: terrestrial animals (including man) and plants

- Day 7: God rested

There are a number of chronic problems with the biblical creation account. Most notably:

- Scientific evidence indicates that the universe was not *created*. It *evolved* over many billions of years.

- Scientific evidence indicates that life was not *created*. It also *evolved* over many billions of years.

- The moon is not a source of light, it only reflects the sun's light.

- Stars are not incidental lights in the night sky, they are actually suns—many of which are much larger than our own.

- It does not explain where God came from.

THE BIBLICAL FLOOD

According to Genesis 6–9, God began to recognize the wickedness of humankind, so, he decided to:

> … blot out from the earth the men whom I created—men together with beasts, creeping things, and birds of the sky for I regret that I made them.

At that time, God directed Noah to build an ark to hold: himself, his wife, his sons, his son's wives, his grandchildren, two of every living creature on Earth, and enough provisions to support them for an extended period of time at sea.

When Noah finished building the ark and loading everyone and all the provisions into it, God made it rain for forty days and forty nights—until the waters covered the tallest mountains. After about eight months, the water finally receded, and Noah's family and all of the animals left the ark to repopulate Earth.

There are *many* improbability issues with the biblical flood account. One of the most improbable relates to the flood itself. Scientists maintain that, throughout most of Earth's history, there has always been about the same amount of water. Water is involved in a continuous cycle from accumulation, to transpiration, and evaporation, to condensation, to precipitation, and then back again to accumulation. This process is known as the hydrologic cycle and is essentially a closed cycle. Heavy local rainfall can cause local flooding, but it cannot raise ocean levels, because evaporated ocean water is the primary source of the condensed water vapor that falls as rain. Therefore, it is not physically possible to raise ocean levels with increased rainfall.

Nevertheless, Genesis 7:20–23 states that the deluge covered the tops of all the mountains, killing every animal on Earth. Assuming that God could, and did, preempt the hydrologic cycle and estimating that the average height above sea level, globally, is around three thousand feet, it would take about five hundred million cubic miles of water to cover the tallest mountains; that is more water than presently exists in all of Earth's oceans, lakes, and ice sheets combined.

It would have to rain 650 feet, all day, every day, everywhere on Earth, for forty days in order for water to cover all of Earth's mountains. Incidentally, the heaviest rainfall ever recorded over a one hour period, was twelve inches, in Holt, Missouri on June 22, 1947.[60] Twelve inches of rain in an hour is very heavy rainfall, *but it would have to have rained twenty-seven feet every hour of every day for forty days to reach the levels described in Genesis.*

If the entire Earth were covered with water, the oceans' salt water and the land's fresh water would have mixed, rendering all water on Earth, at least temporarily, too salty for freshwater creatures and not salty enough for sea creatures to survive in. Additionally, when the waters evaporated,[61] they would have deposited enough salt on Earth's surface to render its soil too salty to sustain most of the terrestrial plant life that exists here today.

Another improbability issue relates to the ark. Many proponents of the biblical flood myth maintain that the ark was built more in the form of a box than of a ship. If so, that would have maximized the space within the dimensional parameters allegedly set forth by God, but the vessel would not have been as structurally sound as a typical ship's hull. Nevertheless, this form will be used to calculate how much wood would have been required

---

60 http://wmo.asu.edu/world-greatest-sixty-minute-one-hour-rainfall

61 The biblical flood could not recede, because there was no place for the waters to recede to.

to build the ark, as well as its capacity to hold all of Earth's animals and enough food to sustain them for more than eight months.

God allegedly instructed Noah to make the ark three hundred cubits long (450 feet) by fifty cubits wide (seventy-five feet) by thirty cubits high (forty-five feet), with a bottom and two decks. A vessel that size would have required more than 110,000 board feet of lumber[62] to build: or enough wood to build about thirty-five three-bedroom ranch-style homes. That is a lot of lumber to process even with a sawmill, which Noah and his sons obviously did not have. In fact, they did not have saws, or even iron tools. In the twenty-first century BCE, the only tools that would have been available to them would have been primitive stone and bronze hand tools.

In regard to the dimensions of the ark, its proponents insist that engineers have determined it would have been an "extremely seaworthy vessel." However, before steel ships were built, wooden ship builders experimented with a number of large hull designs and determined that the practical maximum length for wooden ships, even ones built with modern tools and technologies, was less than 150 feet. Wooden ships longer than that were built and tested, but all of them failed to perform adequately. Even in moderate seas, they flexed too much to remain watertight and required constant pumping to stay afloat.

There are also a number of "experts" who, after "careful calculations," have determined that the ark was large enough to hold all of Earth's animal species, but that claim is absurd. It is not known exactly how many living animal species exist on Earth, but estimates range from between two to ten million.[63] Assuming that each deck of the hypothetical ark contained about 22,500 square feet (the maximum possible), one deck, for example, would only have provided about 0.096 square feet for each pair of the known living

---

62 These are estimates assuming four-inch-thick planking was used for the sheathing and decking, and two-inch-thick planking was used for the building of approximately 750 six-feet-square compartments on the bottom and middle decks.

63 These estimates do not include extinct species, which are estimated to represent more than 99 percent of the total number.

species of beetles. That doesn't leave much room for all of the other known living animal species and the food to sustain them for eight months at sea.

Understandably, proponents of the biblical flood never address the survival of terrestrial plant species. This is almost certainly because few, if any, of them could have survived being submerged in water for eight months. Where, one might wonder, did the dove that Noah released from the ark after the waters receded find an olive branch?

These are just a few of the multitude of improbability issues related in the Tanakh. When its content is evaluated objectively, it becomes abundantly clear that it cannot be taken literally, and as such, cannot be regarded as divine.

THE HOLY BIBLE (CHRISTIANITY)

Most Christians believe that Jesus established Christianity, but that is not true. Jesus led a movement initiated by John the Baptist, after John was executed around 30 CE.[64] That movement later became know as the "Jesus movement," but Christians must realize that *Jesus was a devout Jew* and that the Jesus movement was a *Jewish* movement. Christianity was actually established (after Jesus was executed) primarily by a Roman Jew named Paul, *who did not know and never met, Jesus.*

The Christian religious text is the Holy Bible. It contains:

• The Old Testament, and

• The New Testament

The Old Testament is the Jewish Tanakh. It has been reordered and modified slightly to serve Christian premises better, but it is essentially the same book. The reason for its inclusion in the Holy Bible is complex, and it may represent the most egregious act of plagiarism ever committed.

---

64 There is no consensus on the date of John's death. For example, Josephus, the Jewish historian, places it much later than most biblical sources.

In any event, like Jews, Christians believe that the Old Testament contains the actual laws of God—as provided by God to Moses 3,300 years ago. However, Christians believe they have been absolved from adherence to those laws through **antinomianism**, a concept Paul explained in the New Testament (Romans 3:20, 3:28, etc.).

Consequently, it is the New Testament that defines Christianity, and it has a very convoluted history. The oldest known version of the New Testament is in a copy of the Holy Bible know as the Codex Vaticanus, which was written in Greek sometime in the fourth century CE. Actually, there never was an original New Testament. Different versions of it evolved independently over relatively long periods of time in different areas. Nevertheless, the supporters of each version maintain that *their* version is the *correct* version.

Regardless of the version, the New Testament deals with the birth, life, teachings, death, and resurrection of Jesus. Its existence is remarkable because virtually nothing was written about Jesus during his lifetime.

The New Testament is composed of twenty-seven books, including:

- Four Gospels (outlining Jesus's life),

- Acts (a narrative of the apostles' ministries),

- Twenty-one Epistles (letters written to different churches in the Roman Empire), and

- Revelation (an apocalyptic prophecy).

These books have been attributed to a number of different authors. But many objective religious historians maintain that no one actually knows who wrote much of the New Testament.

What Christians *believe* they know about Jesus comes primarily from the four canonical Gospels: Matthew, Mark, Luke, and John. But no one knows exactly when the Gospels were written—or even who wrote them. Most objective scholars, however, agree that they were written thirty to eighty years after Jesus died. As for their authorship, there is more disagreement, but it is doubtful that any of the authors actually knew Jesus, witnessed his activities, or listened to his sermons.

The primary purpose of the canonical Gospels was to demonstrate that Jesus was the Jewish Messiah and to promote his divinity. That was accomplished by citing his lineage back to King David and the events in his life that fulfilled Old Testament (Jewish) prophecies.

There were many other Christian Gospels available for canonical consideration, but they were rejected. In 185 CE, Irenaeus (bishop of Lyons) selected Matthew, Mark, Luke, and John as *the* canonical Gospels. In *Adversus Haereses*,[65] he explained why. *These passages are admittedly difficult to read, but they are very important because they established which gospels would be the Canonical Gospels—and the Canonical Gospels form the backbone of the Holy Bible and Christianity:*

> Matthew: Now the Gospels, in which Christ is enthroned, are like these…Matthew proclaims his human birth, saying, "The book of the generation of Jesus Christ, son of David, son of Abraham," and, "The birth of Jesus Christ was in this manner"…for this Gospel is manlike, and so through the whole Gospel [Christ] appears as a man of a humble mind, and gentle.

> Mark: Now the Gospels, in which Christ is enthroned, are like these…But Mark takes his beginning from the prophetic Spirit who comes on men from on high saying, "The beginning of the gospel of Jesus Christ, as it is written in Isaiah the prophet," showing a winged image of the gospel. Therefore he made his message compendious and summary, for such is the prophetic character.

> Luke: Now the Gospels, in which Christ is enthroned, are like these…That according to Luke, as having a priestly character, began with the priest Zacharias offering incense to God. For the

---

65 http://www.ntcanon.org/Irenaeus.shtml#4_Gospels

fatted calf was already being prepared which was to be sacrificed for the finding of the younger son.

John: Now the Gospels, in which Christ is enthroned, are like these…For that according to John expounds his princely and mighty and glorious birth from the Father, saying, "In the beginning was the Word, and the Word was with God, and the Word was God," and, "All things were made by him, and without him nothing was nothing made." Therefore, this Gospel is deserving of all confidence, for such indeed is his person.

The Gospels could not possibly be either more or less in number than they are. Since there are four zones of the world in which we live, and four principal winds, while the Church is spread over all the earth, and the pillar and foundation of the Church is the gospel, and the Spirit of life, it fittingly has four pillars, everywhere breathing out incorruption and revivifying men. From this it is clear that the Word, the artificer of all things, being manifested to men gave us the gospel, fourfold in form but held together by one Spirit. As David said, when asking for his coming, "O sitter upon the cherubim, show yourself." For the cherubim have four faces, and their faces are images of the activity of the Son of God. For the first living creature, it says, was like a lion, signifying his active and princely and royal character; the second was like an ox, showing his sacrificial and priestly order; the third had the face of a man, indicating very clearly his coming in human guise; and the fourth was like a flying eagle, making plain the giving of the Spirit who broods over the Church. Now the Gospels, in which Christ is enthroned, are like these.

Irenaeus believed that he was able to determine that these particular Gospels were the *correct* Gospels, because he recognized their

"God-breathed," or "Spirit-breathed," contents. Christian clerics maintain that scripture is inspired by God, and that they can recognize its divinity. They cite 2 Timothy 3:16 in defense of their claim:

> All scripture is given by inspiration of God, and is profitable for doctrine, for reproof, for correction, for instruction in righteousness.

Like many religious claims, this one is both improbable and unverifiable, but it is also impossible to disprove.

"TRUTH"

Before proceeding any further, it is important to explain that the Abrahamic religious concept of "truth" is different than the social definition that we are accustomed to.

Because all Abrahamic religions believe their doctrines are essentially divine, they also believe they represent immutable truths. The ramifications of this interpretation are significant, because their doctrines also maintain that the successful dissemination of their versions of the truth—no matter how it is achieved—is righteous. That attitude has led to the perpetration of a great many unjust acts. They occur in all religions, but more so among the many Christian denominations. In any event, it is important to realize that Abrahamic religious dogmas do not have to be true in order for them to be regarded as "truths."

FIVE CHRISTIAN TENETS

The Gospels of Matthew, Mark, Luke, and John may have been chosen for their "spirit-breathed" content, but coincidentally, they also most closely supported the orthodox beliefs of Irenaeus and other second-century church clerics. Orthodox Christianity rests on five indisputable tenets, that Jesus:

- was born of a virgin;

- was the rightful king of Judea;[66]

- died for our sins;

- was resurrected and ascended into heaven; and

- will return one day to rule Earth.

And one fundamental assumption, that:

- Paul received guidance from Jesus after Jesus's death.

Any Gospel, book or letter, regardless of its source, that supports these premises is regarded by Christians as true, and any that does not support them is regarded as false or heretical.

PAUL THE "DISCIPLE"

Paul was a Pharisee Jew with Roman citizenship, who, as an adult, converted to the aristocratic Sadducees. Initially, Paul vehemently opposed the messianic movement that Jesus was involved in. However, when traveling to Damascus several years after Jesus died, Paul allegedly fell from his horse and had a vision where Jesus instructed him to:

> make thee a minister and a witness both of these things which thou hast seen, and of those things in the which I will appear unto thee. (Acts 26:13–14)

---

66 That Jesus is the rightful king of Judea, according to orthodox Christians, is demonstrated by his alleged fulfillment of Old Testament prophecies.

At that time, Paul joined the messianic Jewish movement Jesus had led when he was alive and began to minister to Roman and Greek Gentiles. Jesus's disciples apparently supported Paul's ministry to the Gentiles—but not what he taught. His messages, although captivating, did not conform to the messianic movement that John the Baptist and Jesus led. Listed below are some examples. Paul initiated the concepts that:

- Jesus died for humankind's sins (1 Corinthians 15:3).

- Jesus was buried and rose again on the third day (1 Corinthians 15:4).

- Jesus ascended to heaven (Romans 8:34).

- Jesus will return to rule over Earth (1 Thessalonians 4:13–18).

Paul also taught the following:

- Those who accepted the atonement of Jesus's sacrifice would be given eternal life (1 Corinthians 15:51–54 and 1 Thessalonians 4:13–18).

- The Lord's Supper, or Eucharist, identifies wine as Christ's blood, bread as Christ's flesh, etc. (1 Corinthians 3:16–17 and 11:23–28).

And most disturbing to Jesus's disciples was that Paul claimed that the Laws of Moses no longer had to be observed:

Wherefore the law was our schoolmaster to bring us unto Christ, that we might be justified by faith. But after that faith is come, we are no longer under a schoolmaster. (Galatians 3:24–25)

There can be little doubt that Paul devoutly believed in his mission, and was almost solely responsible for creating Christian premises 3, 4, and 5—that Jesus:

- died for humankind's sins;

- was resurrected and ascended into heaven; and

- will return one day to rule Earth.

Although Paul promoted the movement that evolved into Christianity—using Jesus as its figurehead—it is important to remember that Jesus, his disciples, and his followers were devout Jews, not Christians. Consequently, Paul did not promote the teachings of Jesus according to Jesus; *he promoted the teachings of Jesus according to Paul.* Regardless of how improbable Paul's claims were regarding his relationship with Jesus, *Christendom is based upon them.*

JESUS'S MESSAGE

None of Jesus's sermons were recorded during his lifetime, so we do not know exactly what he said. Nevertheless, it is believed by many religious historians that his brother James continued to preach the same messages after Jesus was executed (Tabor 2006, 272–277). If that was the case, then we should look to the Book of James for insights into the teachings of Jesus. The date of authorship of James is unknown, but most historians believe James actually did write or recite the passages attributed to him. Consequently, it may be both the earliest and most credible representation of the messianic movement Jesus was involved in. James's messages were rather plain and ordinary, but they are far more consistent with first-century messianic Jewish doctrine than Paul's.

James addressed: devotion and obedience to God, fairness to others, caution in speech, the risks of wealth, and the virtues of patience and prayer. Pertinently, though, he never addressed virgin births, the Eucharist, divinity, Jesus returning to Earth, or eternal life. *Nor is there any other reliable source of information to suggest that Jesus or his followers ever endorsed or promoted those beliefs.*

THE HISTORICAL JESUS

There is a plethora of information claiming similarities between the story of Jesus's life and the lives of earlier mythological pagan man-gods, such as Mithra, Osiris, Krishna, Dionysus, Buddha, etc. It is pertinent to recognize that Jesus was not the first man-god who allegedly possessed more than two of the following traits:

- born of a virgin

- born on December 25

- birth was attended by wise men/angels

- performed miracles

- died for the salvation of humankind

- resurrected on or around the spring equinox

- ascended into heaven/nirvana

- promised to return one day to rule Earth

An innovative disputation of these pagan precedents was offered by the second-century Christian **Apologist** Saint Justin Martyr. When confronting their similarities, he stated:

> I am established in the knowledge of and faith in the Scriptures
> by those counterfeits which he who is called the devil is said to
> have performed among the Greeks; just as some were wrought
> by the Magi in Egypt, and others by the false prophets in

Elijah's days. For when they tell that Bacchus, son of Jupiter, was begotten by [Jupiter's] intercourse with Semele, and that he was the discoverer of the vine; and when they relate, that being torn in pieces, and having died, he rose again, and ascended to heaven; and when they introduce wine into his mysteries, do I not perceive that [the devil] has imitated the prophecy announced by the patriarch Jacob, and recorded by Moses? And when they tell that Hercules was strong, and traveled over all the world, and was begotten by Jove of Alcmene, and ascended to heaven when he died, do I not perceive that the Scripture which speaks of Christ, "strong as a giant to run his race," has been in like manner imitated? And when he [the devil] brings forward Sculapius [the god of medicine] as the raiser of the dead and healer of all diseases, may I not say that in this matter likewise he has imitated the prophecies about Christ? (Chapter LXIX)

And:

Perseus was begotten of a virgin; I understand that the deceiving serpent counterfeited also this. (Chapter LXX; from Justin Martyr's Dialogue with Trypho)

In other words, Martyr claimed the devil was able to anticipate not only the coming of Jesus but also the conditions surrounding his birth, life, death, and resurrection—and imitate them thousands of years before they actually occurred. Additionally, it is significant that Martyr didn't question the historicity of these individuals—only their originality. Remarkably, he was defending the biblical account of Jesus even before the canonization of the New Testament.

Since Jesus wasn't the original man-god with these attributes, should his story also be regarded as myth rather than fact? *In truth, very little is known about Jesus.* Nevertheless, most historians believe that a Galilean Jew named Jesus did exist, and that he:

- was born between 7 and 2 BCE in Nazareth;

- preached a messianic form of Judaism to small groups of mostly disenfranchised Jews;

- may have believed he was the rightful king of the Jews;

- overturned the tables of the money changers in Herod's Temple during Passover; and

- was arrested for sedition and crucified by the Romans sometime between 27 and 36 CE.

However, there is no evidence or reason to believe Jesus:

- was born of a virgin;

- was accompanied by wise men or angels at his birth;

- performed miracles;

- died to save humankind;

- was resurrected;

- ascended into heaven; or

- will return one day to rule Earth.

The historical Jesus is very different from the biblical Jesus. It is everyone's right to believe as he or she chooses, but the belief in the biblical Jesus is definitely an irrational belief.

The earliest mention of Jesus in a historical context occurs in the Antiquities of the Jews by Josephus, a prominent first-century Jewish historian. The earliest surviving copies of that text are in Greek from the eleventh century. They read:

> Now there was about this time Jesus, a wise man if it be lawful to call him a man, for he was a doer of wonderful works—a

teacher of such men as receive the truth with pleasure. He drew many after him both many of the Jews, and many of the gentiles. He was [the] Christ; and when Pilate, at the suggestion of the principal men among us, had condemned him to the cross, those that loved him at the first did not forsake him, for he appeared to them alive again the third day, as the divine prophets had foretold these and 10,000 other wonderful things concerning him; and the tribe of Christians, so named from him, are not extinct at this day.[67]

The authenticity of this passage has been questioned for many hundreds of years, because it conforms to Christian rather than Jewish ideology. The earliest extant copies of this volume are from Christian sources, so it is generally believed the passages promoting Jesus as the Son of God were added to it. Many Jewish scholars believe the original text actually read:

Now there was about this time Jesus, a wise man, for he was a doer of wonders. He drew many after him. When Pilate, at the suggestion of the principal men among us, had condemned him to the cross, those that loved him at the first did not forsake him, and the tribe of Christians, so named from him, are not extinct at this day.[68]

It can be inferred from the absence of recorded information regarding Jesus's life during his lifetime that he was not regarded as an important personage at that time. Nor, more importantly, is there any indication that anyone considered him divine until long after he died. The New Testament was the initial source for that tenet: through Paul's epistles and the virgin birth accounts in Matthew 1:18–25 and Luke 1:27–35.

The canonical Gospels appear first in the New Testament, but it is generally agreed that some of Paul's epistles preceded them chronologically.

67 http://religiousstudies.uncc.edu/people/jtabor/josephus-jesus.html
68 http://religiousstudies.uncc.edu/people/jtabor/josephus-jesus.html

Paul's letters are not usually regarded as source material for the authors of the Gospels, but the possibility that they were aware of, and influenced by, Paul's letters should be considered.

DIVINITY

Critical to Christian belief is the tenet that Jesus was conceived by God and born of a virgin. It is also one of the most contentious issues of Christianity. In Matthew 1:18–25, Mary's pregnancy is addressed. This is how it appears in the King James Version of the Holy Bible:

> Now the birth of Jesus Christ was on this wise: When as his mother Mary was espoused to Joseph, before they came together, she was found with child of the Holy Ghost.
>
> Then Joseph her husband, being a just man, and not willing to make her a public example, was minded to put her away privily.
>
> But while he thought on these things, behold, the angel of the LORD appeared unto him in a dream, saying, Joseph, thou son of David, fear not to take unto thee Mary thy wife: for that which is conceived in her is of the Holy Ghost.
>
> And she shall bring forth a son, and thou shalt call his name JESUS: for he shall save his people from their sins.

This passage is interpreted by Christians as a fulfillment of the following prophecy in Isaiah 7:14:

> Therefore the Lord himself shall give you a sign: Behold, a virgin shall conceive, and bear a Son, and shall call his name Immanuel.

In the earliest Greek versions of the New Testament, the term *parthenos* (virgin) is used, but in the earliest Masoretic (Jewish) texts (which are generally considered to be the more accurate), it is given as *almah* (young woman). Additionally, the context of Isaiah 7:14 is completely inappropriate for addressing the coming of a future messiah. Consequently, that "tenet" may have resulted from the mistranslation of a word and the misinterpretation of a prophecy.

POSSIBLE ORIGIN OF THE VIRGIN BIRTH MYTH

Each calendar year, there are four significant, annual celestial events that affect seasons: the spring equinox (equal day and night), the summer solstice (longest day–shortest night), the fall equinox (equal day and night), and the winter solstice (shortest day–longest night).

In the Northern Hemisphere, on the shortest day of the year, the Sun rises in the constellation Virgo ("the Virgin"). That event has traditionally been used to identify the beginning of the winter solstice or, more pertinently, when days begin to lengthen. It has also been referred to variously as the "birth of the sun," and the "day when the virgin gives birth to the sun."

Currently, the winter solstice occurs on December 21, but several thousand years ago, due to the precession of the equinoxes (see Appendix), it occurred on December 25. This is an important distinction, because at that time, nearly all man-gods in mythology were born of a virgin on December 25 (the winter solstice). Coincidence?

In truth, no one knows when Jesus was born, but there is absolutely no reason to assume or believe that he was born on December 25, or that he was born of a virgin. [69]

DISSENTION

Since the inception of Christianity, there has been a great deal of dissention regarding the relationship between God, Jesus, and the Holy Spirit. In 325

---

[69] http://paganizingfaithofyeshua.netfirms.com/no2_virgin_birth_sun_myth.htm

CE, in an attempt to address those issues, Emperor Constantine headed a council at Nicea attended by three hundred bishops, priests, and deacons.

The council proclaimed that God (the Father), Jesus (the Son), and the Holy Spirit were actually one godhead. This arrangement is known as the Trinity, and it enabled Jesus to be divine and still eligible for Judean kingship.[70]

Establishing the Trinity was intended to unify Christendom, which in some ways it did. However, disagreements regarding whether the Holy Spirit came from the Father and the Son, or just the Father polarized Christians into two separate factions that eventually led to the division of Christendom into eastern (Greek Orthodox) and western (Roman Catholic) factions in 1054 CE.

Christianity is regarded as a single religion, but that is a mistake. Since the primary division in 1054 CE, it has split into thousands of smaller polarized factions. It is unlikely that there will ever be a consensus among Christians regarding Christianity because, like the geocentric astronomical model, it is based on impossible precepts.

THE QURAN (ISLAM)

The Muslim religious text is the Quran. It is composed of:

- Thirty parts, with

- One hundred and fourteen chapters

Islam became a formal religion in the seventh century CE with the teachings of Muhammad. However, Muslims maintain that Islam is not a new religion at all, but a revival of the ancient religion practiced by Adam, Abraham, Moses, Jesus, and other biblical prophets. Muslims believe God

---

70 http://www.mgr.org/ConstantinePart1.html

commanded Muhammad to *re*establish his true laws—laws that had been corrupted through time by Jews and Christians.

Muslims claim that every copy of the Quran is exactly the same. That may be true for copies written in Arabic, but it is certainly not true for English translations of the Quran—they vary enormously. Some emphasize the peaceful nature of Islam, and some emphasize its aggressive, violent, and warlike nature.

In light of these discrepancies, it was decided that the contents of the Quran could not be evaluated objectively. Consequently, its history alone has to be relied upon to provide insights into its potential credibility.

MUHAMMAD

The Quran is essentially a compilation of revelations allegedly received by Muhammad—from God—through the angel Gabriel over a twenty-three-year period of time. Muhammad:[71]

- 570: was born in Mecca (Saudi Arabia)[72]

- 576: was orphaned and raised by his uncle Abu Talib

By all accounts, Muhammad's early life was unremarkable. He tended flocks for the Meccans and may have occasionally accompanied his uncle on journeys to southern Arabia and Syria.

- 595: married a rich widow (more than twice his age) named Chadidja

The marriage provided him with the affluence to spend much of his time alone and in contemplation in the mountains near Mecca.

---

71 http://www.thereligionofpeace.com/pages/history.htm
72 There are no Muslim dates prior to 622 CE.

- 610: allegedly received his first revelation from God when meditating in a cave on Mount Hira.

Muhammad claimed that the angel Gabriel appeared to him and commanded him, in the name of God, to promote the true religion that would be revealed to him.

- 614: began to preach his revelations publicly

Initially, Muhammad's preaching was tolerated by the Meccans, but in time, Muhammad alienated them and was driven away.

- 622: immigrated to Medina with a group of his followers

There, Muhammad allegedly continued to receive revelations from God and became a powerful leader. This transition is recognized as paramount in Islam and marks the beginning of the Islamic calendar (Islamic year 1 corresponds to 622 CE in the Christian Gregorian calendar).

- 624: claimed to have received permission from God to wage war against the "enemies of Islam" (22:39–40).

- 624: led a small force of Muslims who defeated a much larger force of Meccans at Badr

This victory increased Muhammad's status and power throughout the region.

- 624: evicted Qaynuqa Jews from Medina, confiscating all of their property

- 624: ordered the assignation of Abu Afak (a Jewish poet who questioned Muhammad)

- 624: ordered the assignation of Asama bint Marwan (a Jewish woman who spoke out against Muhammad)

- 624: ordered the assignation of Ka'b al Ashraf (A Jewish poet who spoke out against Muhammad)

- 625: evicted Banu Nadir Jews from Medina

- 627: massacred Qurayza Jews at Medina

- 628: made a pilgrimage to Mecca

- 628: subjugated Khabar Jews

- 628: sent emissaries with written demands to foreign leaders to acknowledge him as a divine prophet and to accept Islam as their faith

Muhammad's messengers met with varying degrees of success, but the Christian leader Amru the Ghassanide held so much contempt for Muhammad's demands that he executed the emissary.

- 629: responded to this insult by sending three thousand troops against Amru, but Amru, with help from the Greeks, was able to repel the Muslim advance and drive them back

That was the first of many conflicts that would occur between Christians and Muslims. Muhammad's defeat encouraged the Meccans to break faith with him and prompted them to commit several acts of violence against his allies.

- 630: responded to their transgressions by invading and capturing Mecca with ten thousand soldiers

At that point in time, the Meccans agreed to acknowledge Muhammad as their leader and prophet, which established Islam as the dominant religion in Arabia.

- 631: dies

Muslims maintain that Muhammad proffered peace, but history reveals that his life was very violent. Additionally, it appears that the wide-spread acceptance of Islam was accomplished with considerable force.

RECORDING THE QURAN

According to orthodox Muslims, God's revelations were memorized by Muhammad and then recited to his followers, who also memorized and/or recorded them. This unstructured approach at preserving the Quran was initially considered acceptable.[73] After the Battle of Yamama, though, in 633 CE, so many Muslims who had memorized portions of the Quran were killed that Abu Bakr, the first **caliph**, ordered that it to be compiled into a single body of written text. That was reportedly accomplished within six months of Muhammad's death—but it was not organized into its present form at that time.

That didn't happen until Uthman ibn Affan, the third caliph, recognized the need for standardization. He organized a committee who produced the version known as the Uthmanic Codex. It was completed sometime between 650 and 656 CE. At that time copies of it were sent to all of the Muslim provinces, where Muslim scribes began to make more exact copies of it. It was also at that time that Uthman ordered all previous copies of the Quran, in whole or in part, destroyed.

Muslims claim the current version of the Quran is identical to the original Uthmanic Codex, and that it contains, quite literally, the actual words of God spoken to Muhammad through the angel Gabriel in the 600s CE, but that claim is unlikely to be true.

Several existing Quran manuscripts, specifically the Samarqand and Topkapi copies, are believed by many Muslims to be original Uthman texts, but many scholars challenge that assumption, because they were written in a type of script that was not generally used before the late 700s CE.

---

73 Cultures in this region apparently were very skilled at memorizing large volumes of text, lineages, poetry, etc.

Additionally, in 1972, during renovation of the Great Mosque of Sana'a in Yemen, tens of thousands of fragments of text from some of the earliest known copies of the Quran were recovered—some of which exhibited discrepancies from today's Quranic texts.

The earliest extant versions of the Quran date from the late 700s CE. Consequently, like Jews and Christians, Muslims are not in possession of their original scripture or an undisputed, accurate facsimile of it.

RELIGIOUS CONTENTION

POLARITY

The histories of Judaism, Christianity, and Islam are histories of contention and violence. Adherents of these religions have been killing each other continually to maintain and/or expand their influences since their inceptions. This is truly puzzling because Jews, Christians, and Muslims all believe in the same God, recognize most of the same prophets and angels, and share a common ancestry.[74] So, why does so much animosity exist between them? In order to answer that question, we have to go back and look at the Torah from a slightly different perspective.

No one actually knows who wrote the Torah or when it was written. Scholars, however are fairly certain that it was written by more than one individual—over an extended period of time. Regardless of who wrote it, or when it was written, it contains extremely polarizing sentiments. The first of which is that:

- God favors Jews over all other people:

  For thou art a holy people unto HaShem thy God, and
  HaShem hath chosen thee to be His own treasure out of all

---

74 Jews and Christians do not recognize Muhammad as a prophet.

peoples that are upon the face of the earth (Deuteronomy 14:2, et al.).

The second is that:

- God regards Gentiles (specifically Egyptians and Arabs) with contempt. Anti Egyptian/Arab sentiments occur throughout the Torah, most notably: Abraham's rejection of his half Egyptian son, Ishmael (Genesis 21: 9-16), God wrecking havoc on the Egyptians with plagues (Genesis 7-12), and even God helping, the Israelites to "smite" various Arab tribes in their conquest of Canaan (Exodus 32: 27-19, et al.).

These assertions naturally offended Gentiles and severely alienated them.

By the first century CE, some Europeans in the Mediterranean region were ready to adopt monotheism, but because Gentiles had been regarded as inferior to Jews in the Torah, they could not adopt Judaism. However, when Paul introduced Christianity, a new monotheistic religion that recognized the same god as the Jews—regarded everyone as equals—offered an afterlife in heaven—and didn't require great personal sacrifice, it caught on very quickly.

Christians incorporated the Jewish Tanakh into their bible to enhance Jesus' credibility, but then immediately nullified it through antinomianism. In so doing, they offended Jews and severely alienated them.[75]

Additionally, by including the Tanakh in their religious text, Christians tacitly supported the Jewish claim that Egyptians and Arabs were inferior to Jews in the eyes of God—inadvertently offending and severely alienating them.

---

75 Some solidarity now exists between Jews and Christians—but only because they share a more threatening common adversary: Islam.

By the seventh century CE, Muhammad was willing to adopt monotheism, but because Egyptians and Arabs had been demeaned by Jews and Christians, he established a new religion, Islam.

When Muhammad established Islam, he accepted the Jewish god, Yahweh as the "one true god." He also incorporated all of the Jewish prophets and angels from the Tanakh into Islam. However, he claimed that the Tanakh was a corruption of God's laws and that God had provided *him* with the "true" laws so that *he* could reinstate them. This claim naturally offended Jews and permanently alienated them.

Muhammad also acknowledged the existence of Jesus, but regarded him as a prophet, not the Son of God. In so doing, he offended Christians and permanently alienated them.

Despite all of the polarity that exists today, most Jews, Christians, and Muslims can coexist. Unfortunately, fundamentalist adherents of these faiths righteously believe that:

- *their* religious texts define the *one true* religion as established by God,

- other faiths are actually false religions engendered by the devil, and that

- adherents of other faiths are enemies of God, and therefore, their enemies.

Consequently, as long as Abrahamic religions exist, there will be irresolvable contention between them.

Similar contentions exist between different sects *within* Judaism, Christianity, and Islam, and there are many of them. According to the Religious Tolerance website, for example, there are about *thirty thousand* recognized Christian sects.[76] Unfortunately, fundamentalist adherents of these sects righteously believe that:

---

76 http://www.religioustolerance.org/christ7.htm

- *their* interpretations, of *their* versions, of *their* religious texts define the *one true* religion as established by God,

- other faiths are actually false religions engendered by the devil, and that

- adherents of other faiths are enemies of God, and therefore, their enemies.

Chronic conflict betweens sects of the same religion seems unlikely, but it is actually very prevalent. Within Christendom, for example, Protestants and Catholics have been killing each other for centuries—the same holds true with Sunni and Shia Muslims— even Jesus' arrest (and eventual execution) occurred as a result of ideological polarity between Pharisee and Sadducee Jews.

Perhaps the most pertinent consideration regarding polarity between religions, and religious sects within religions, is that by their own definitions, *only one of them can be right, which logically means that all the rest of them must be wrong.* To put these numbers in perspective, the odds against anyone actually choosing the right sect—of the right religion is only about 0.003 percent. And according to most of them, the consequences of choosing incorrectly can be dire, indeed.

CONFLICT

Beyond evaluating the credibility of Abrahamic religious texts, it is pertinent to also evaluate Abrahamic religious conduct, because it is determined, to a large degree, by scriptures within their texts.

There is a long history of conflict between Jews and Egyptians as well as Jews and Arabs (both as pagans and as Muslims). This is unfortunate, but not particularly surprising because they live in close proximity to each other. The dynamics behind conflicts between Muslims and Christians, however, is far more complex.

For four hundred years after the establishment of Islam, Muslims expanded their influence in the Mediterranean region. Christians had been reasonably successful in preventing their encroachment into Western Europe, but by the end of the eleventh century, Muslims had taken possession of most of North Africa and the entire Middle East, including Jerusalem.

Jerusalem was traditionally the Jewish Holy City, but Christians and Muslims both came to regard it as a sacred place integral to their faiths. Christians, because Jesus was crucified there and Muslims because Muhammad once prayed there. The Jewish claim to Jerusalem is arguably much stronger than the Christian claim, and the Christian claim is arguably much stronger than the Islamic claim.

Nevertheless, all of these faiths traditionally regarded Jerusalem as the place where God lived, so they fought continuously to gain or maintain control of it. Christian crusaders from as far away as England even got involved in the fracas. Tragically, throughout its turbulent history, Jerusalem has been completely destroyed twice, besieged twenty-three times, attacked fifty-two times, and captured and recaptured forty-four times![77] Clearly this is a city that has been sought after obsessively to its detriment.

In any event, the Islamic occupation of Jerusalem provoked Western involvement in the region. It is unlikely that the United States would ever have become directly involved in this conflict if it weren't for two mitigating circumstances: first, there is a lot of oil in the Middle East that the United States wants, and second, we actively supported the founding of the Jewish state of Israel along the eastern shore of the Mediterranean Sea—in direct opposition to Arab-Muslim interests. Since then, the United States has not been well regarded there by anyone but the Israelis.

Relationships worsened in 1953 when the United States became involved in a coup d'état that overthrew the democratically elected Iranian Prime Minister, Mohammad Mosaddegh. He was replaced with a

---

77 http://en.wikipedia.org/wiki/History_of_Jerusalem

pro-western Iranian general named Fazlollah Zahedi, so that Britain and the United States could maintain control of Iranian oil.

The United States further alienated Arab Muslims in 1979 when President Jimmy Carter granted political asylum to Mohammad Reza (the oppressive Shah of Iran) after he had been overthrown. In protest, Iranian students and militants took over the US Embassy in Tehran, capturing 52 Americans and holding them hostage until after the Shah died of cancer in 1980.

Relationships worsened even further in 1990 after Iraqi officials announced that Kuwait was stealing up to three hundred thousand barrels of Iraqi crude oil each day.[78] Kuwait was allegedly accomplishing that theft through wells drilled diagonally across their common border—with US support.[79] The Iraqi leader, Saddam Hussein warned Kuwait to stop—and announced to the rest of the world that they would not tolerate the theft of their oil.

According to Iraqi officials, Kuwait did not stop, so the Iraqi army entered Kuwait and destroyed the offending wells. The important consideration here is that if the accusation was true, then the invasion was arguably justified.

Whether the invasion was justified or not, the Iraqi occupation of Kuwait was regarded as very threatening to Saudi Arabia, because its top-producing oil fields were adjacent to Kuwait's. That meant that they were within striking distance of Hussein's forces if he decided to invade Saudi Arabia as well. The United States also regarded this situation as threatening because we relied on access to that oil.

Saudi military forces were formidable, but they were no match for Iraq's. Consequently, an extremist Saudi Sunni Muslim named Osama bin Laden offered his services to King Fahd of Saudi Arabia to bolster his defenses.

---

78 http://www.rense.com/general3/slant.htm

79 To my knowledge, it has never been ascertained whether this claim was true or not.

Bin Laden maintained an army that had been instrumental in repelling the Soviet invasion in Afghanistan, so his offer was legitimate. However, for a number of complex political reasons, Fahd rejected bin Laden's offer and instead agreed to allow the United States to station troops in Saudi Arabia—allegedly to provide them with protection and to drive the Iraqi forces out of Kuwait.

Consequently, the United States used Saudi Arabia as a staging area to launch strikes against Saddam Hussein's forces. Former president George H. W. Bush claimed that our involvement was primarily altruistic, but our motive for being there was clearly to protect our access to Middle Eastern oil.

Strategically, it was a logical move, but placing our troops in Saudi Arabia inadvertently offended and angered bin Laden and other fundamentalist Muslims. Unbeknownst to us at that time, even the temporary occupation of Saudi Arabia by infidels was regarded by them as an unforgivable transgression.

Up until then, the United States had been dealing primarily with old-fashioned greed. But once bin Laden became involved, that changed. We were then dealing with fundamentalist religious zealotry. On September 11, 2001, bin Laden responded to our "transgressions" by having a number of passenger jets hijacked and flown into important US edifices—namely, the World Trade Center buildings in New York City and the Pentagon in Washington, DC.

We know that the al-Qaeda attacks were instigated by individuals reacting to circumstances in accordance with extremist Islamic indoctrination, but what about our responses to those attacks? Did we react objectively, or did we react in accordance with our own religious indoctrination?

In response to the attacks, former president George W. Bush decided the best course of action was to invade Iraq, a country, as it turns out, that had no direct involvement in the terrorist attacks. We don't know why Bush decided to invade Iraq, but his response to a question posed by Bob

Woodward in a 2004 interview is revealing. When asked if he had solicited advice from his father,[80] Bush responded:

> His earthly father was "the wrong father to appeal to for advice... there's a higher father that I appeal to" (Woodward 2004).

It is not illogical to assume from this statement that Bush believed that God advised him to invade Iraq. If so, there can be little doubt he believed he was serving God's will—but, then again, so probably did bin Laden when he directed the 9/11 attacks against the United States.

It is extremely disconcerting to realize that former president George W. Bush and Osama bin Laden prayed to the same god for guidance.

MORALITY

Without religious laws, religions claim that people would revert to beastly behavior. Religions certainly want us to believe that dogma, because it ensures continuing support for themselves and helps to validate their existence. But is it true?

It is impossible to answer that question definitively, because none of us has ever lived in a society without religions. Consequently, we do not know exactly how we would behave without them. However, religions did not invent moral behavior; they only recognized admirable behavior in humans, defined it as moral, and then claimed jurisdiction over it.

Moral behavior is probably intrinsic to all of us, just as it is to all animal species. If there were no laws to abide by, most of us would still behave morally. In fact, our behavior might actually improve if we adhered to our consciences rather than religious directives. Additionally, although most religious doctrines do advocate moral behavior, they do not behave morally

---

80 George H. W. Bush opted not to invade Iraq when he had the opportunity during the first Gulf War. Additionally, George W. Bush did not think it was necessary to consult with either Secretary of State Colin Powell or his Cabinet members before making the decision to invade Iraq (Woodward 2004).

themselves. Over the last two thousand years, in an effort to maintain and expand their influences, religions have been responsible for the perpetration of more injustice and violent behavior than any other artificial cause.

MOTIVES

If religions do not save souls and do not induce moral behavior, what purpose do they serve? Arguably, none. Many millions of people insist that their religions provide them with some degree of solace. But if the solace is from irrational fears of a devil and hell instilled in them by their religions, then that argument is moot.

Some churches do provide services to, and beyond, their communities. However the primary motivation of religion's is to expand their influences within and beyond their societies. Toward that end, religions work diligently to solicit and indoctrinate new members so that they will contribute to their support.

There is no way to know how much financial support religions receive each year, because they do not have to report their incomes. However, just in the United States, there are about 160 million[81] adult Christians. If each of them donates four hundred dollars a year, Christianity receives about $64 billion annually—just from donations. To put that amount in perspective, it is more than Exxon-Mobil and General Electric, the two largest US corporations, *made together* in 2007. This estimate may be high or low, but one way or the other, religions receive an enormous amount of financial support from adherents each year. Remarkably, they do this without having to pay taxes.

Religions receive tax-exempt status from many governments (including our own) partly because leaders in administrations have been indoctrinated to support them, and partly because no leader—in any administration—in any government—in any but the most oppressive regimes could survive

---

81 http://www.adherents.com/

without tacit approval from the dominant religions in their societies. Consequently, political leaders will generally not risk alienating them— regardless of their personal beliefs.

IMPACT

Religions are generally regarded as essentially positive entities in our societies, but that assumption needs to be challenged. When their merits and demerits are evaluated objectively, a valid case can be made that their net affect is actually negative. Religions offer little more than unverifiable promises of everlasting salvation—in an unverifiable place called heaven. But they encourage anthropocentric attitudes that contribute to severe damage to other species and the environment, and ethno-centric attitudes that incite inter-religious polarity and conflict. That they are held in such high regard is not a testament to their intrinsic value, but to how well they have been promoted.

Part III: Environmental Degradation

We abuse land, because we regard it as a commodity belonging to us. When we see land as a community to which we belong, we may begin to use it with love and respect.

—Aldo Leopold

8: Environmental Change

*Technology…is a queer thing. It brings you great gifts with
one hand, and it stabs you in the back with the other.*

—Carrie P. Snow

Environmental change is a natural process that occurs continuously on
Earth, because Earth is a dynamic planet in a dynamic universe. Most
of the change that has taken place since Earth was formed has increased
opportunities for species development and diversification—but not all of
it. Paleontologists maintain that 99.99 percent of the plant and animal
species that have ever existed on Earth have gone extinct—mostly due to
environmental change.

A myriad of natural forces, ranging from volcanic eruptions to asteroid
impacts, affect Earth's environment, and these influences can be gradual or
instantaneous, gentle or cataclysmic, local or global.

Species themselves inadvertently modify their environments, simply
by existing. The most notable example of this occurred during the Archean
Era beginning about 2.8 billion years ago. At that time, the atmosphere
was anaerobic and unsuitable for life as we know it. Then something truly
remarkable happened: cyanobacteria (blue-green algae) began to draw sustenance from sunlight, carbon dioxide, and water and expel oxygen into
the atmosphere: a process known as photosynthesis. Over the next billion
years, cyanobacteria gradually oxygenated Earth's atmosphere, making it

possible for more advanced life-forms to develop but, ironically, far less suitable for them.[82]

Although all species impact Earth's environment to one degree or another, only one—humans, especially civilized humans—seriously, adversely impact it. Artificial development has and is severely damaging Earth's environments.

82 http://www.scientificamerican.com/article.cfm?id=origin-of-oxygen-in-atmosphere

9: Land Development

*Because we don't think about future generations, they will
never forget us.*

—Henrik Tikkanen

In order to accommodate our "needs," we build cities and towns with complex infrastructures of interstates, highways, roads, and railways to connect them. We build dams, aqueducts, and pipelines to supply our cities and towns with water and electricity. We pump oil and gas out of the ground and build pipelines to transport it. Nearly everything we do negatively impacts Earth's environments. But no aspect of artificial development wreaks greater havoc on the environment than agriculture.

AGRICULTURE

The extent to which agriculture negatively impacts environments depends partly on the specific agricultural practices employed—but more so on the percentage of land claimed for its use. Estimates vary, but currently, about 28 percent of Earth's most productive land is devoted exclusively to agriculture. Approximately 30 percent (3.6 billion acres) of that total is cropland, and 70 percent (8.5 billion acres) is pasture. Only 5 percent (0.6

billion acres) of it is irrigated, but that 5 percent produces about 40 percent of our food.[83]

Once land is claimed for agricultural use, current agricultural practices mandate that only a very few select plant species are grown there. Other plant species that attempt to establish themselves are generally killed through cultivation or with poison. Wild animal species are likewise discouraged from utilizing this land by restricting their access to it or killing them as well. This type of exclusivity in land use is practical, because it maximizes crop yields and profits, but it is extremely detrimental to other plant and animal species.

Our population is currently about 6.7 billion and is expected to reach 9.2 billion by 2050.[84] Supporting the additional 2.5 billion people will require that we claim an additional four billion acres of land and devote it exclusively to crop production. If we allow that to happen, our impact on the environment will be catastrophic. Claiming that much of Earth's productive land will inevitably lead to the extinction of thousands of plant and animal species, adversely affect most others, and diminish our long-term survival prospects.

Irresponsible agricultural practices exacerbate this problem. An increasingly large percentage of claimed land is used to grow crops—to feed livestock—to feed people. As we become more affluent, we tend to rely more heavily on protein from animals than plants. Aside from the fact that this trend is unhealthy for us, it is devastating to the environment.

Approximately 70 percent of rain forests being cleared in the Amazon today, for example, are being cleared to create rangeland for livestock. Typically, the life span of that rangeland is less than ten years. Rain forest topsoil is typically very shallow and quickly depleted. Once it is depleted, that land frequently turns into unproductive desert. Consequently, hundreds of thousands of acres of lush rain forest are permanently destroyed each year so that we can have cheap beef. [85]

83 http://www.pbs.org/earthonedge/ecosystems/agricultural1.html

84 http://geography.about.com/od/obtainpopulationdata/a/worldpopulation.htm

85 http://www.converge.org.nz/pirm/ofow.htm

Additionally, according to the Livestock, Environment and Development Initiative, livestock currently contributes 9 percent of the carbon dioxide and 37 percent of the methane emissions worldwide—meaning that approximately 18 percent of the total global greenhouse gas emissions are produced by livestock.[86]

Clearing rain forests to create rangeland to raise more beef is profoundly stupid. Rain forests provide environments for a wide variety of critical biota, they convert massive amounts of carbon dioxide into oxygen through photosynthesis, and they store immense amounts of carbon in their trunks and limbs. When rain forests are logged and burned, all of those benefits are lost—in many cases, effectively, permanently. We not only allow this environmental travesty to occur, we support it by purchasing cheap imported beef.

Additionally, meat production is far less efficient than plant production. For instance, it takes seventy-eight calories of fossil fuel to produce one calorie of protein from beef, but only two calories of fossil fuel are needed to produce one calorie of protein from soybeans. More than 30 percent of our resources (including fossil fuels) are now devoted to livestock production.[87]

Paradoxically, agriculture is our greatest achievement and our greatest nemesis. If we are going to survive as a species, *as agriculturalists*, we will have to adopt far more responsible agricultural practices.

86 http://woods.stanford.edu/cgi-bin/focal.php?name=livestock&focal_area=land_use_and_conservation

87 http://www.converge.org.nz/pirm/ofow.htm

10: Water Diversion

We never know the worth of water till the well is dry.

—Thomas Fuller

Our impact on aquatic environments is also significant. We drain wetlands and swamps, dam and move rivers, and even connect oceans with canals.

One of our most audacious accomplishments—and the one that, linked with agriculture, has been most responsible for the widespread success of artificial development—is water diversion: the transfer of water from one location to another.

Water diversion usually entails building dams that produce reservoirs. Water is diverted out of the reservoirs through artificial canals to other locations, sometimes far from its natural destination.

Currently, there are about forty-eight thousand dams over fifty feet high worldwide. Collectively, they impound about 1,439 cubic miles of water (which is more water than is in Lake Michigan). These reservoirs provide water for irrigation, domestic use, the generation of electricity, and habitat for certain types of aquatic wildlife.[88] However, they severely inhibit the flow of 135 of Earth's 227 largest rivers. So much water is diverted from

---

88 http://wwf.panda.org/what_we_do/footprint/water/dams_initiative/quick_facts/

them, that eight of Earth's largest rivers no longer always reach their natural outlets. They are the: [89]

- Colorado River (United States and Mexico)

- Rio Grande River (United States and Mexico)

- Indus River (Pakistan)

- Amu Darya River (Russia)

- Syr Darya River (Russia)

- Yellow River (China)

- Teesta River (Sikkim)

- Murray River (Australia)

The eventual consequences of damming Earth's major rivers are unknown. However, dams are directly responsible for the degradation of many major riparian ecosystems. Civilization has benefitted enormously from water diversion projects over the short-term, but there are already indications that these short-term benefits will be offset by long-term environmental problems.

Even so, it is unlikely that many dams will be removed. But it is a certainty, if civilization is to persevere, that they will have to be modified to lessen their damaging impacts.

---

89 http://environment.nationalgeographic.com/environment/photos/rivers-run-dry/#/
freshwater-rivers-murray-1c_46634_600x450.jpg

11: Pollution

The use of solar energy has not been opened up, because the oil industry does not own the sun.

—Ralph Nader

POLLUTANTS

One of the chronic negative side effects of artificial development is the proliferation and dispersal of pollutants. As a result, we have, in a very short period of time, managed to poison all of Earth's air, most of its water, and much of its soil. There are literally no places left on Earth where we can breathe air that does not contain various chemical pollutants, and there are few places on Earth where surface water is still potable. Pollution is a major problem associated with artificial development that adversely impacts Earth's environments and diminishes our long-term survival prospects. In this discussion, pollution will be regarded as harmful concentrations of:

- organic waste

- natural chemicals

- synthetic chemicals

Chemists divide chemicals into two main groups. Those that contain carbon are regarded as organic, and those that do not are regarded as inorganic. These designations were established in the eighteenth century when chemists mistakenly believed that carbon-based chemicals contained some mysterious essence of life (Bryson 2003, 99). That conclusion turned out to be wrong, but by the time it was realized, the terms had become firmly established.

Chemists have no problem dealing with these incongruities, but it is very confusing for laypeople to grasp the concept that chemicals such as chlorpyrifos, dichlorvos, tetrachlorvinphos, and azinphos-methyl are organic—especially since they are not and never have been alive, do not exist in nature, and were developed specifically to extinguish life.

The use of these terms is further complicated when addressing the topic of pollution, because pollutants are also regarded as organic and inorganic. Consequently, if using them, we would be forced to address, for example, inorganic pollutants composed of organic chemicals. Fortunately, these confusing incongruities can be avoided by using the aforementioned terms for pollutants, organic waste, natural chemicals, and synthetic chemicals.

ORGANIC POLLUTANTS

Organic pollutants are harmful concentrations of organic contaminants, such as: human sewage, runoff from feedlots, slaughtering by-products, lawn clippings, etc. It is important to realize that these contaminants are natural and are generally not considered pollutants, unless they occur in *un*natural concentrations *and* enter groundwater.

Organic contaminants, even in unnatural concentrations, do not generally pose problems as long as they remain on, or in, soil. They eventually break down and enrich it—making it more fertile. When unnatural concentrations of organic contaminants enter groundwater, however, they become pollutants and can be very destructive. In groundwater, organic contaminants rob dissolved oxygen from water that is needed by fish and other aquatic organisms to survive. When oxygen levels fall below five parts per million (ppm), the effects on aquatic life in streams, rivers, lakes, and oceans can be devastating. These areas produce, and sustain, much of Earth's aquatic biota, so when their productiveness is diminished, it adversely affects many other species as well.

There are two important conditions moderating the impact of organic pollution. Its negative effects are generally local. And although they may be temporarily devastating, if the causation is eliminated, the effected biota will generally recover completely.

NATURAL CHEMICAL POLLUTANTS

Natural chemical pollutants are harmful concentrations of chemicals that occur in nature, such as: arsenic, lead, copper, mercury, phosphate, methane, ammonia, nitrite, nitrogen, phosphorus, carbon dioxide, etc. In natural concentrations, these chemicals generally are not harmful. However, in unnaturally high concentrations—such as those sometimes created through artificial development—they can present serious health risks and adversely affect habitats.

Some natural chemicals, specifically those used in fertilizers, have relatively short-term effects on the environment—similar to those of organic pollutants. However, the negative effects of metallic chemicals—such as plutonium, lead, arsenic, and mercury—are, for all practical purposes, permanent.

SYNTHETIC CHEMICAL POLLUTANTS

Synthetic chemical pollutants are harmful concentrations of chemicals produced by humans in laboratories that do not exist in nature. The most prominent of these are: dioxins, polychlorinated biphenyls (PCBs), insecticides, fungicides, and herbicides. Because these chemicals do not exist in nature, there is concern that they may eventually prove to be more toxic to organisms than natural chemicals. As of yet, however, there is no conclusive evidence to corroborate that concern. Nevertheless, a number of synthetic chemicals, such as the insecticide dichlorodiphenyltrichloroethane (DDT) and PCBs, have proved to be so toxic that it is now illegal to manufacture or use them. Additionally, the most toxic chemicals—dioxins such as 2,3,7,8-tetrachlorodibenzo-p-dioxin (TCDDs)—are not intentionally manufactured and have no useful applications at all. They are actually accidental by-products created by the combustion of chlorine-based chemical compounds with hydrocarbons. The production of bleached paper and polyvinyl chloride (PVC) plastics is a major source of dioxins—as are commercial waste incineration projects and even backyard burn barrels.[90]

Synthetic chemical pollutants can be extremely harmful, even in very small concentrations. Additionally, like some natural chemical pollutants, they tend to be very durable, allowing them to accumulate over time in soil, water, and the atmosphere. One of the most alarming aspects of using synthetic chemicals is that their negative side effects frequently do not manifest themselves until long after they have been widely dispersed. For example, chlorofluorocarbons (CFCs) were developed in the late 1920s as a "safe" alternative to the toxic gases then used in refrigeration units, but the fact they destroyed ozone in the stratosphere was not discovered until the mid-1970s.[91]

Ozone absorbs harmful ultraviolet radiation in Earth's atmosphere, so even its partial destruction can be extremely detrimental to Earth's biota. Remarkably, a single chlorine atom released from CFCs in the stratosphere can destroy one hundred thousand ozone atoms, so the release of massive amounts of CFCs into the atmosphere was seriously depleting Earth's protective ozone layer. Fortunately, that condition was recognized and acted upon responsibly, so by 1987, the production of CFCs had been banned. Current research indicates that the ozone layer is gradually restoring itself.

90 http://www.ejnet.org/dioxin/
91 http://www.esrl.noaa.gov/gmd/hats/publictn/elkins/cfcs.html

These are just a few examples of the damaging effects synthetic chemicals have had on Earth's environments. It is unlikely that many of them will ever cause serious problems. However, it is probable that some of them that are now believed to be safe will eventually turn out to have equally detrimental side effects.

MONSANTO

Many chemical manufacturers act irresponsibly when it comes to the manufacturing, storage, and dispersal of the chemicals they produce but few more so than Monsanto.

Unless otherwise noted, the following information was obtained from the GMWatch website.[92] By the mid-1970s, Monsanto had developed a very bad reputation for producing two highly toxic chemicals that were proving to be serious environmental pollutants: dioxin, and PCBs. Because of irresponsible production, distribution, and application of these chemicals, Monsanto was plagued by persistent cleanup costs and lawsuits. Listed below is a compilation of some of these issues:

- 1987: Exposed litigant in a $180 million settlement for Vietnam War veterans to Agent Orange

- 1991: Fined $1.2 million for trying to conceal the discharge of contaminated wastewater

- 1995: Ordered to pay $41.1 million for hazardous waste dumping

- 1995: Ranked fifth in EPA's Toxic Release Inventory among US corporations for discharging thirty-seven million pounds of toxic chemicals into the air, land, water, and underground

---

92 http://www.gmwatch.org/gm-firms-mobile/10595-monsanto-a-history

- 1997: Reported by the *Seattle Times* to have sold six thousand tons of cadmium-contaminated waste to Idaho fertilizer companies

- 2002: Published an article in the *Washington Post* titled "Monsanto Hid Decades of Pollution, PCBs Drenched Ala. Town, But No One Was Ever Told"

Monsanto began production of PCBs in 1929. Developed to cool transformers, it was soon found to be useful in other applications as well. For more than fifty years, PCBs were carelessly produced, stored, and used, so traces of them are now found in virtually every living creature on Earth. Unfortunately, PCBs were also found to be one of the most toxic chemicals ever created. PCB pollution was particularly severe in the town of Anniston, Alabama, where much of it was produced. According to the *Washington Post*:

> For nearly forty years, while producing the now-banned industrial coolants known as PCBs at a local factory, Monsanto Co. routinely discharged toxic waste into a west Anniston creek and dumped millions of pounds of PCBs into oozing open-pit landfills. And thousands of pages of Monsanto documents— many emblazoned with warnings such as "CONFIDENTIAL: Read and Destroy"—show that for decades, the corporate giant concealed what it did and what it knew.

Regarding the risks of PCBs, the US Environmental Protection Agency (EPA) states:

> PCB has been demonstrated to cause cancer, as well as a variety of other adverse health effects on the immune system, reproductive system, nervous system and endocrine system.

In 1968, after internal testing of the effects of PCBs, Monsanto set up a committee to assess its options. The results of the study were never made public—at least not until the *Abernathy v. Monsanto* trial in 2002, when 3,600 plaintiffs from Anniston claimed the Monsanto plant located there knowingly contaminated its community with PCBs. The report concluded that:

> the evidence proving the persistence of these compounds
> and their universal presence as residues in the environment is
> beyond question…the public and legal pressures to eliminate
> them to prevent global contamination are inevitable.

The *Guardian* newspaper reported Monsanto's internal response to those findings:

> The subject is snowballing. Where do we go from here? The
> alternatives: go out of business; sell the hell out of them as long
> as we can and do nothing else; try to stay in business; have
> alternative products.

In 1969, the company wrote a confidential paper titled the "Pollution Abatement Plan," which admitted:

> The problem involves the entire United States, Canada, and
> sections of Europe, especially the UK and Sweden.

There is no doubt that Monsanto knew about the problems associated with PCBs and did nothing to alleviate them. Eventually, the company was found guilty of conduct:

> so outrageous in character and extreme in degree as to go
> beyond all possible bounds of decency so as to be regarded as
> atrocious and utterly intolerable in civilized society.

By the time the Anniston pollution case came to court, Monsanto had already been divided into two corporations—Monsanto and a new company called Solutia. Monsanto and Solutia collectively agreed to pay $600 million to the more than twenty thousand Anniston residents adversely affected by Monsanto's irresponsible practices. However, Monsanto quickly distanced itself from Solutia, leaving the latter with billions of dollars of environmental cleanup costs and other liabilities—liabilities that it obviously could not meet. Solutia was forced to declare bankruptcy in 2003, and Monsanto was absolved of all responsibility.

A strong case can be made that Solutia was established fraudulently—solely to protect Monsanto.

AIR POLLUTION

LEAD

Lead is an extremely dangerous toxin. In children, it damages the brain and nervous system, is responsible for behavioral and learning problems, impairs growth, and causes deafness and headaches. In adults, lead poisoning causes reproductive problems in men and women, high blood pressure, hypertension, nervous disorders, memory and concentration problems, and muscle and joint pain.[93] There is no getting around the fact that lead is bad for us, and once it is introduced into our bodies, it never leaves, because it is an accumulative poison.

Unfortunately, before its toxicity was recognized, lead was used in many household products—including paint, water pipes, solder used to seal tin cans, and most unfortunately, gasoline.

One of the biggest problems associated with internal combustion motors in the early 1900s was formulating gasoline mixtures that did not ignite prematurely under compression. Engineers knew that improved performance could be attained with higher-compression motors, but they could not find fuels that did not ignite spontaneously under increased compression. Such fuels caused engines to "knock."

---

93 http://www.epa.gov/lead/pubs/leadinfo.htm#facts

Then, in 1921, while working for the General Motors Research Corporation in Dayton, Ohio, a researcher named Thomas Midgley, Jr. began to experiment with a gasoline additive called tetraethyl lead. Tetraethyl lead turned out to be the miracle additive that the automotive industry had been waiting for. It boosted **octane** levels considerably with only a nominal increase in cost (Bryson 2003, 149).

Leaded gasoline was important in the development of more efficient and powerful internal combustion motors, and it was a boon to many industries. At that time, lead was known to be a neurotoxin, but it *did* stop engines from knocking, so in 1923, General Motors, DuPont, and Standard Oil of New Jersey began to produce and market leaded gasoline, or as it was more commonly known then, "Ethel" (Bryson 2003, 150).

For the next thirty years, the world blissfully burned enormous quantities of leaded gasoline. Then, in the 1950s, an American chemist and geologist named Clair Patterson, who was measuring lead isotope levels in rock samples, noticed that they were always contaminated with large amounts of atmospheric lead. Patterson decided to investigate the phenomenon and discovered that lead concentrations in human bones had increased more than five-hundred-fold since the early 1920s. He also determined, through innovative ice core studies, that there was *no* lead in the atmosphere before its introduction into gasoline in 1923.

Patterson realized that leaded gasoline was slowly poisoning everyone on Earth. In 1970, he announced his findings before a special US Senate hearing. Producers of leaded gasoline, automobile manufacturers, and even the US government vehemently contested the information he presented. Consequently, petroleum corporations were allowed to continue producing leaded gasoline, even though they knew its use was adversely affecting all of us. Eventually, however, good judgment prevailed, and in 1973, the Environmental Protection Agency (EPA) called for a gradual phase down of leaded gasoline, and in 1996, it was removed from gasoline completely.[94]

---

94 http://www.epa.gov/aboutepa/history/topics/lead/02.html

Lead is just one of many thousands of chemical pollutants that are carelessly introduced into Earth's atmosphere every day, most of which, unfortunately, don't have conscientious researchers monitoring them. *We all owe a huge debt of gratitude to Clair Patterson. He singlehandedly fought some of the most powerful US corporations to get lead removed from gasoline—and prevailed. His contribution to the welfare of all biota on Earth cannot be overstated. It was enormous.*

CARBON DIOXIDE

The air pollutant of greatest concern today is carbon dioxide. Carbon dioxide is not normally considered a pollutant; in fact, life could not exist without it. However, by definition, when any chemical occurs in harmful concentrations, it must be regarded as a pollutant, and that is definitely the case now with carbon dioxide.

Enormous amounts of carbon dioxide are artificially emitted into the atmosphere by burning fossil fuels, clearing forests, making cement, livestock production, and other activities intrinsic to civilized existence.

Ice core studies indicate that the normal, pre-industrial revolution level of atmospheric carbon dioxide was about 280 parts per million (ppm). Today it is almost 400 ppm and rising every year.

Many researchers believe that increasing levels of atmospheric carbon dioxide from human pollution are responsible for a current warming trend in Earth's climate. This is a reasonable assumption, because humans are introducing large volumes of carbon dioxide into the atmosphere, it is an insulating greenhouse gas, and temperatures are rising—especially in the northern hemisphere.

There can be little doubt that carbon dioxide pollution is exacerbating this problem. However, the issue is far more complex than it seems.[95]

---

95 Climate change is beyond the scope of this discussion to address in detail, but more information about it is provided in the Appendix for those who would like to know more about it.

Geologists maintain that major, long-term climate change is actually determined by three celestial cyclic events:

- the eccentricity of Earth's orbit around the sun

- variations in Earth's axial tilt

- the precession of Earth's axis around its geographical center

These cycles are known collectively as the Milankovitch Cycles,[96] and they are responsible for determining Earth's major glacial and interglacial climatic episodes. (See Appendix for more information regarding the Milankovitch cycles.)

Within glacial and interglacial episodes are cooling periods known as stades and warming periods known as interstades. Stades and interstades are caused by:

celestial events (increasing or decreasing sun spot activity, meteor impacts, etc.),

- terrestrial events (volcanic eruptions, increasing or decreasing atmospheric insulation, etc.), and

- other presently unknown conditions.

In any event, although stades and interstades can profoundly influence Earth's climate, their affects are generally, *relatively* short-term (fig. 4).

The dotted line in the graph shows Earth's temperature increase due to the Milankovitch cycles since the Late Glacial Maximum (LGM) eighteen thousand years ago, while the solid line shows the fluctuations in Earth's actual mean temperatures due to stades and interstades over the same time period.[97] It is important to realize that Earth's temperature increased by more than 6° C (10.8° F) between the LGM and the Industrial Revolution

96 Named for the Serbian mathematician Milutin Milanković, who first calculated their effects on Earth's climate

97 Determined from ice core studies in Greenland

without any human intervention. Consequently, it is impossible to know whether, or how much of, the 0.7° C (1.26° F) increase that has occurred since then is attributable to the present interglacial or an interstade caused by human pollution.

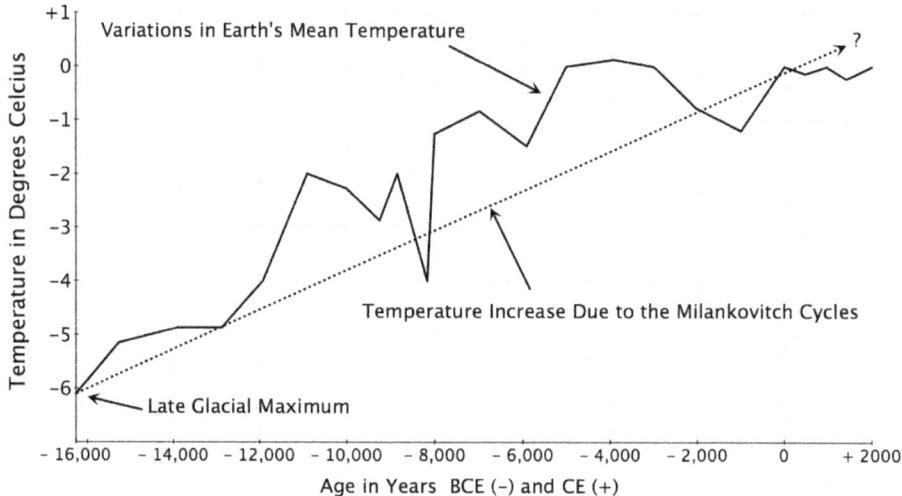

Figure 3: Variations in Earth's temperature since the LGM

From a geological perspective, a 0.7° C (1.26° F) increase is neither abnormal nor particularly alarming. What is alarming, however, is that the global mean temperature is now at a critical level. If it continues to increase, many of Earth's most productive ecosystems, such as savannas and plains, could become too arid to support the rich array of biota they presently do. Additionally, Antarctic ice would begin to melt, raising ocean levels and inundating coastlines. The melting fresh water would also dilute the salinity of Earth's oceans, which would drastically affect **thermohaline** circulation, impacting marine environments in ways that are beyond our ability to predict.

In other words, an additional increase of only a few degrees in Earth's mean temperature, regardless of the cause, could drastically, negatively impact Earth's environments. This means that whether human pollution is responsible for global warming or only exacerbating it, we must curb it.

Not doing so would be catastrophic for many species of plants and animals, including our own.

WATER

CHEMICAL FERTILIZERS

In the past, many industrial pollutants were released directly into streams, rivers, lakes, and oceans. Today, that practice is prohibited in most advanced countries, but it is still a serious problem in Third World countries. The most pervasive water pollutants are undoubtedly agricultural fertilizers that accumulate in streams, rivers, lakes, and oceans. Chemical fertilizers enable farmers to produce far more crops than they could otherwise, but their negative impacts on Earth's aquatic organisms are profound.

Most chemical fertilizers are composed of nitrogen (N), phosphorus (P), and potassium (K). Nitrogen fertilizers promote plant growth, but nitrogen is very soluble and does not bond with soil particles. Consequently, it frequently finds its way into groundwater as nitrates.[98] Once nitrates enter streams, rivers, lakes, and oceans, they provide algae with greatly increased growth potential. Algal growth promotes bacterial growth, and bacterial growth robs dissolved oxygen from the water.

As with oxygen depletion caused by organic pollution, the loss of oxygen caused by nitrates reduces the capacities of water systems to support healthy populations of aquatic organisms.

The problems associated with chemical fertilizers stem primarily from the quantity of their use. Worldwide, farmers apply more than 165 million tons of them annually.[99] This problem is exacerbated by the fact that farmers, especially those in Third World countries, frequently over-apply fertilizer in an attempt to maximize crop yields.

---

98 http://www.caf.wvu.edu/~forage/nitratepollution/nitrate.htm

99 http://www.pollutionissues.com/A-Bo/Agriculture.html

Consequently, we have a conundrum here. We cannot feed the world without chemical fertilizers, but their use is definitely adversely impacting Earth's aquatic environments. So, once again, we are faced with an aspect of artificial development that is providing short-term survival advantages, while adversely affecting our future prospects. Arguably, anything that damages the environment cannot, in the long run, be beneficial to us. Unfortunately, with rising populations, the use of chemical fertilizers, especially in Third World countries, is likely to increase. Researchers predict that 243 million tons of chemical fertilizers will be applied annually worldwide by the year 2020.[100]

Irresponsible agricultural practices have depleted much of the natural fertility of our agricultural lands. Consequently, farmers must now rely on chemical fertilizers to produce crops. They also, in an attempt to maximize yields and profits, use chemical herbicides to eliminate competing plant species and chemical insecticides to protect their crops from insects.

Utilizing irresponsible agricultural practices—such as these—to increase yields and profits is shortsighted and foolish. Responsible agriculture requires that farmers allow fields to lay fallow, rotate crops, plant cover crops, and add compost and manure to them. However, farmers have found it far more cost effective to forgo these practices in favor of using chemicals. The net effect of employing irresponsible agricultural practices is that we are rendering much of Earth's most productive land less productive than it once was. This means we will have to claim more and more land and rely ever more heavily on chemical fertilizers, herbicides, and pesticides to support us in the future— conditions that severely, adversely affect Earth's environments.

CARBON DIOXIDE

When it comes to concerns regarding carbon dioxide pollution, we have bigger and more immediate problems to deal with than global warming. Carbon dioxide pollution is acidifying Earth's oceans at an alarming rate.

---

100 http://www.pollutionissues.com/A-Bo/Agriculture.html

Earth's oceans absorb about 25 percent of the carbon dioxide introduced into the atmosphere. Scientists have been aware of this condition for a long time and have regarded it as a moderating influence to the harmful effects of atmospheric carbon dioxide pollution. However, when carbon dioxide dissolves in seawater, the water become acidic.[101]

Oceanographers have noted that the rate of ocean acidification since the beginning of the Industrial Revolution has increased enormously. Certainly nothing comparable to it has occurred in the last twenty-one million years. And although the pH of Earth's oceans is not yet severely, adversely affecting marine biota, the projected increase in acidification certainly will (fig. 5).

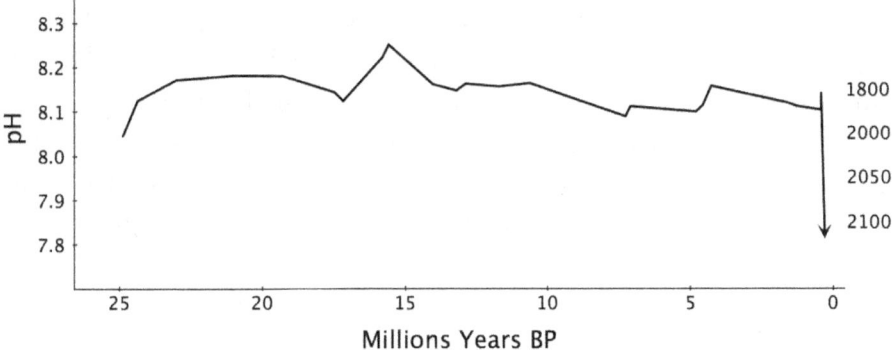

Figure 4: Ocean acidification over the last 21 million years

When carbon dioxide dissolves in seawater, it forms carbonic acid. Carbonic acid releases hydrogen ions, which then combine with carbonate ions to form bicarbonate. Pertinently, many marine creatures rely on carbonate ions to build their shells. Oceanographers predict that, if the increase in acidification and the decrease in carbonate ions continue at

---

101 Unless otherwise noted, the following information in this section was obtained from the Ocean Acidification Network website (http://www.ocean-acidification.net/FAQacidity.html).

their present rate, there will be severe oceanic biota loss by 2050 and near total collapse of biota in many areas of the oceans by 2100.

Regarding concentrations of carbonate ions in oceans, oceanographers recognize two saturation zones. The zone closer to the surface contains sufficient levels of carbonate ions for marine organisms to build their shells, while the colder and deeper zone is naturally unsaturated and acidic enough to dissolve those minerals. The transition between them is called the saturation horizon. The saturation horizon is estimated to have shifted between fifty and two hundred meters upward since the beginning of the Industrial Revolution.

Presently, most scientists believe placing a ceiling on atmospheric carbon dioxide concentrations of 550 ppm—expected by 2050—would avoid severe climate change problems. However, oceanographers are now warning that carbon dioxide concentrations over 450 ppm would begin to eliminate the saturation zones hospitable to marine life from higher- and lower-latitude oceans. Therefore, they are recommending an absolute atmospheric carbon dioxide concentration ceiling of 450 ppm. Alarmingly, at the present rate of increase, that level will be reached by 2030.

SPECIES AFFECTED

Most of the life-forms that would be directly and adversely affected by a lack of carbonic ion saturation in Earth's oceans are minute creatures, such as: coccolithophorids, foraminifera, and pteropods. Their loss or diminishment may not seem that important, but they form the base of the food chain for almost all marine organisms.[102] Their loss, or diminishment—besides being catastrophic to nearly every animal species in the oceans—would also be catastrophic to humans, because we rely on many of the species that rely on those minute organisms for our own survival.

---

102 http://www.global-greenhouse-warming.com/ocean-acidification.html

Additionally, they are responsible for nearly half of the photosynthetic activity on Earth.[103] They produce more oxygen than all of Earth's trees combined, so their loss would contribute enormously to increasing atmospheric carbon dioxide and assumedly, further global warming, and ocean acidification.

LAND

Love Canal is a community named for William T. Love, who envisioned building a utopian community on a tract of land on the eastern edge of Niagara Falls, New York, in the 1890's. Love's plan was to dig a canal between the upper and lower Niagara Rivers where power could be generated cheaply to serve the community.

For a number of reasons, primarily economic, Love's project never progressed beyond digging a huge pit where the canal would have been. In the 1920s, the site was turned into a municipal dump, and in 1942, Hooker Chemical Company purchased it. Between 1942 and 1953, Hooker buried approximately twenty-two thousand tons of hazardous waste in the pit. When it became full, the company covered it with soil and sold it to the city of Niagara Falls for one dollar.[104] In 1955, the 99th Street Elementary School was erected on the site, and hundreds of homes were built around it.

All seemed well until 1976, when unseasonably heavy rains raised the water table and disaster struck. Chemicals began to migrate to the surface throughout the entire neighborhood. Soon afterward, residents were reporting abnormal rates of stillbirths and miscarriages, and many babies were born with birth defects. Alarmingly, when the Agency for Toxic Substances and Disease Registry examined the site, it reported finding 418 types of chemicals in the air, water, and soil at Love Canal—many of which

103 hhttp://www.mbari.org/staff/conn/botany/phytoplankton/phytoplankton_coccolithophorids.htm

104 http://www.library.ucsb.edu/istl/00-spring/article2.html

were toxic, and some of which were known even at that early date to be carcinogens.

Nothing was done about the situation until the spring of 1978, when Dr. Robert P. Whalen, the state health commissioner, declared Love Canal hazardous.[105] In 1979, Eckert C. Beck, administrator of the EPA Region 2 reported:

> I visited the canal area at that time. Corroding waste-disposal drums could be seen breaking up through the grounds of backyards. Trees and gardens were turning black and dying. One entire swimming pool had been popped up from its foundation, afloat now on a small sea of chemicals. Puddles of noxious substances were pointed out to me by the residents. Some of these puddles were in their yards, some were in their basements; others yet were on the school grounds. Everywhere the air had a faint, choking smell. Children returned from play with burns on their hands and faces.[106]

Within a very short period of time, all the residents of Love Canal were evacuated from the area, and the State of New York agreed to purchase the affected homes. Additionally, President Jimmy Carter ordered the Federal Disaster Assistance Agency to assist the City of Niagara Falls in dealing with the Love Canal site problem. However, as Beck reported at that time:

> We suspect that there are hundreds of such chemical dumpsites across this Nation. Unlike Love Canal, few are situated so close to human settlements. But without a doubt, many of these old dumpsites are time bombs with burning fuses—their contents slowly leaching out. And the next victim could be a water supply or a sensitive wetland. [107]

---

105 http://www.library.ucsb.edu/istl/00-spring/article2.html

106 http://www.epa.gov/aboutepa/history/topics/lovecanal/01.html

107 http://www.epa.gov/aboutepa/history/topics/lovecanal/01.html

RESPONSIBILITY

As a result of Love Canal and other hazardous waste site disasters, US Congress passed the Comprehensive Environmental Response, Compensation and Liability Act in 1980, instigating the Superfund project administered by the EPA. With respect to Beck's concerns regarding the number of chemical dump sites across the nation, the EPA stated:

> Over the past 20+ years, Superfund has located and analyzed
> tens of thousands of hazardous waste sites, protected people
> and the environment from contamination at the worst sites,
> and involved states, local communities, and other partners in
> cleanup. Superfund measures its cleanup accomplishments
> through various criterion including construction and post
> construction completions of hazardous waste sites.[108]

There are now 1,300 Superfund sites. According to Scorecard: The Pollution Information Site,[109] approximately eleven million people live within one mile of a Superfund site in the United States. About half of those sites present health hazards to humans, especially through contaminated groundwater or soil. Of the thirty hazardous substances occurring in most of those sites, eighteen are known or are suspected to be carcinogens, and all of them are known to pose serious health risks to humans.

For better or worse, the use of chemicals is an integral aspect of artificial development. Their use enables us to do amazing things that would not be possible without them. But it is important to recognize that many of the chemicals we are producing and utilizing today will eventually prove to have negative side effects. Unfortunately, the negative side effects of many chemicals are not immediately apparent. Consequently, one of the responsibilities of civilized existence is that every generation must be willing to

---

108 http://www.epa.gov/superfund/sites/index.htm
109 http://scorecard.goodguide.com/env-releases/def/land_gen.html

accept responsibility for addressing environmental cleanup issues unintentionally instigated by previous generations.

Currently, our generation is responding responsibly only to environmental issues that directly, adversely affect us now, and we are refusing to accept responsibility for issues that do not. If this evasive attitude prevails, we will be saddling our children with a debt they may not be able to pay—no matter how hard they are willing to try. At the very least, we will be passing on to them a planet with diminished prospects, and at the very worst, a planet that can't be salvaged.

12: Loss of Biota

A true conservationist is a man who knows that the world is not given by his fathers, but borrowed from his children.

—John James Audubon

One of the most disturbing effects of artificial development—at least the current manifestation of it—has been its negative impact on Earth's biota. The International Union for the Conservation of Nature (IUCN) has compiled scientific data on 47,677 species worldwide and has determined that 2 percent of them are already extinct or surviving only in captivity, and that 17,291 of them are regarded as threatened with extinction. This is the most reliable data compiled so far, but Craig Hilton-Taylor, manager of the IUCN Red List Unit, maintains that this information depicts "just the tip of the iceberg," and that "there are many more millions out there that could be under serious threat."[110]

Most biota loss can be attributed to habitat degradation, but overexploitation is responsible for a great deal of it as well.

LOGGING

It would be nearly impossible to overstate the importance of Earth's forests to its terrestrial biota; nearly 90 percent of all species are dependent

110 http://www.iucn.org/about/work/programmes/species/red_list/?4143/Extinction-crisis-continues-apace

upon—and live in—forests. It would also be nearly impossible to understate the negative impact that artificial development has had, and is having, on Earth's forests. At one time, more than 50 percent of Earth's land surface was forested. We have already cut down 80 percent of Earth's old-growth forests—some of which we have allowed to regenerate—but much of the land that was originally forested has been claimed for agricultural use. Consequently, only about 25 percent of Earth is now forested.[111]

Deforestation has been an integral aspect of artificial development for many thousands of years, and it is an activity that has wreaked unimaginable havoc on Earth's biota. It is also an activity that may eventually destroy civilization if not curbed. Deforestation has slowed in some parts of the world—in particular, Europe and North America—but it is escalating in Asia, Africa, and South America. Unfortunately, we are currently cutting down more than sixty thousand square miles of forest every year, and much of that loss is in old-growth rain forests that harbor the greatest amount of biotic diversity. Consequently, the net loss from its destruction is much greater than it seems.

North America and Europe are trending toward reforestation, and although we cannot bring back the old-growth forests or the biodiversity they supported, very positive, recuperative effects are being noted in these temperate zones. Unfortunately, the same degree of recuperation may not be possible in torrid zones. Although these climatic zones are capable of *sustaining* healthy forests, they may not be able to *regenerate* them once they have been cut down. In fact, the end result of deforestation in torrid zones is frequently desertification. When that occurs, the land becomes incapable of sustaining anything more than an impoverished biota.

Besides the detrimental effects that deforestation has on Earth's biota, it also has profound negative effects on Earth's atmosphere and oceans. Trees assimilate enormous amounts of carbon dioxide from the atmosphere and store it as carbon in their trunks and limbs. When they die and decompose,

---

111 http://www.globalchange.umich.edu/globalchange2/current/lectures/deforest/deforest.html

they release that carbon back into the environment. Some of it goes into the ground, but much of it combines with oxygen in the atmosphere, producing carbon dioxide. Some of that carbon dioxide acts as a greenhouse gas (contributing to global warming) and some of it is absorbed by Earth's oceans (contributing to ocean acidification). Additionally, it now appears that deforestation changes local climates. The dynamics behind this phenomenon are not well understood, but nearly every region on Earth that has been deforested now receives less rainfall than it did before its forests were cut down.[112]

HUNTING

Hunting can be broken down into three broad categories based on motives: subsistence, commercial, and sport.

SUBSISTENCE HUNTING

Subsistence hunting was an integral part of our ancestors' foraging subsistence strategies. It also enabled humans to move from torrid to temperate climatic zones. Subsistence hunting undoubtedly, occasionally led to the extinctions of species, but in natural states of existence, the extinctions of species must be regarded as aspects of natural selection. The same is not the case with commercial hunting.

COMMERCIAL HUNTING

Commercial hunting is an activity unique to artificial development and civilized existence. It has been responsible for many species' extinction, but unlike subsistence hunting, extinction resulting from commercial hunting is the result of artificial, not natural, selection.

---

112 http://www.magicalliance.org/Forests/deforestation_decreases_rainfall.htm

One of the most notable examples of species extinction from commercial hunting is the passenger pigeon from the northeastern United States during the first half of the nineteenth century.

PASSENGER PIGEONS

Historians estimate there were somewhere between three and five billion passenger pigeons residing in the eastern North America before it was settled by Europeans. Samuel de Champlain reported seeing "countless numbers" of them in 1605, and Cotton Mather described a flock about a mile wide that took several hours to pass overhead.[113] Flocks that large might seem improbable to us today, but John James Audubon, one of America's most respected ornithologists, reported in the autumn of 1813:[114]

> I left my house at Henderson, on the banks of the Ohio, on my way to Louisville. In passing over the Barrens a few miles beyond Hardensburgh, I observed the Pigeons flying from north-east to south-west, in greater numbers than I thought I had ever seen them before, and feeling an inclination to count the flocks that might pass within the reach of my eye in one hour, I dismounted, seated myself on an eminence, and began to mark with my pencil, making a dot for every flock that passed. In a short time finding the task which I had, undertaken impracticable, as the birds poured in countless multitudes, I rose, and counting the dots then put down, found that 163 had been made in twenty-one minutes. I traveled on, and still met more the farther I proceeded. The air was literally filled with Pigeons; the light of noon-day was obscured as by an eclipse, the dung fell in spots, not unlike melting flakes of snow; and the continued buzz of wings had a tendency to lull my senses to repose.

113 http://www.si.edu/encyclopedia_si/nmnh/passpig.htm
114 http://www.ulala.org/p_pigeon/audubon_pigeon.html

Whilst waiting for dinner at YOUNG'S inn at the confluence of Salt river with the Ohio, I saw, at my leisure, immense legions still going by, with a front reaching far beyond the Ohio on the west, and the beech-wood forests directly on the east of me.

Before sunset, I reached Louisville, distant from Hardensburgh fifty-five miles. The Pigeons were still passing in undiminished numbers, and continued to do so for three days in succession. The people were all in arms. The banks of the Ohio were crowded with men and boys, incessantly shooting at the pilgrims, which there flew lower as they passed the river. Multitudes were thus destroyed. For a week or more, the population fed on no other flesh than that of Pigeons, and talked of nothing but Pigeons.

Native Americans undoubtedly subsistence hunted passenger pigeons for thousands of years, but their populations did not suffer until the 1830s, when Euro-American hunters began to net and shoot them commercially. By 1860, their population was definitely on the wane, and yet commercial hunters continued to pursue them relentlessly.

In 1878, at a large nesting site near Petoskey, Michigan hunters reportedly killed more than seven million passenger pigeons in five months. By the early 1890s, they had been almost completely wiped out in that state. In 1897, a bill was passed in Michigan that banned hunting passenger pigeons for ten years, but by then, it was already too late. There were too few left to reestablish—or even maintain—a viable population.

This same thing has happened to many other species around the world. People seem incapable of exercising restraint when it comes to over-hunting. Perhaps this tendency stems from our age-old instinct to over-harvest in times of plenty to survive winter seasons in temperate climatic zones. As foragers in natural states of existence, however, technological restraints limited how many animals could be harvested, but artificial development has provided us with the means to grossly overharvest. In any event, once again, we are looking at behavior that may have been appropriate in a natural state of existence that is not—or is no longer—appropriate in a civilized state of existence.

SPORT HUNTING

Many environmentalists do not understand or condone sport hunting. However, they should realize that sport hunting does not generally contribute to loss of biota. In fact, sportsmen contribute a great deal of time and money to preserving wildlife and wildlife habitat. The perspectives of environmentalists and sport hunters may differ, but their concerns for the preservation of wildlife and the environment are actually far more likely to coincide than collide.

COMMERCIAL FISHING

Earth's oceans have been exploited for thousands of years. Unlike terrestrial exploitation from logging, farming, mining, etc., however, marine exploitation is not readily apparent. On the surface, an overly exploited ocean looks no different than a healthy one. However, there is now irrefutable evidence that commercial fishing has drastically reduced the populations of nearly every harvestable species of marine organism.

In 1989, a record 95 million tons of fish was harvested worldwide. Since then, there have been significant declines—especially in the Atlantic, Pacific, and Mediterranean oceans. In 1994, crashes in haddock, cod, and yellowtail flounder populations, once thought to be inexhaustible, prompted officials to close six thousand square miles off the coast of Massachusetts to commercial fishing.[115]

The same conditions prevail nearly everywhere. The populations of all species of harvestable marine organisms are declining—rapidly. According

---

115 http://www.converge.org.nz/pirm/frames/fish!f.htm

to a 1995 report by the United Nations (UN) Food and Agriculture Organization (FAO), the "situation is globally non-sustainable, and major ecological and economic damage is already visible."

Another study conducted by twelve scientists from the United States, Canada, Sweden, and Panama concluded that there may be a "global collapse" of harvestable species by 2050.[116]

The scientists involved in the study admit that their dire predictions are not definitive. However, Boris Worm of Dalhousie University in Nova Scotia, the leader of the investigation, stated in an interview that "there is not a piece of evidence" to contradict this prediction. According to Worm, they:

> extracted all data on fish and invertebrate catches from 1950 to 2003 within all 64 large marine ecosystems worldwide... [which] produced 83 percent of global fisheries yields over the past 50 years.

When Worm analyzed the data from the study and extrapolated it into the future, he found it indicated a "100 percent collapse" by 2048. At first, he did not believe the results, but after rechecking all of the data and calculations, he felt compelled to state:

> I don't have a crystal ball, and I don't know what the future will bring, but this is a clear trend...there is an end in sight, and it is within our lifetimes.

On a positive note, there have been some national and international restrictions placed on fisheries to protect specific species of fish, but tragically, the reaction of many nations has been to encourage the building of larger and more efficient boats to harvest diminishing populations more affectively. Nevertheless, researchers believe that if comprehensive

---

116 http://www.nytimes.com/2006/11/03/world/americas/03iht-fish.3383558.html

restrictions were initiated and enforced, many, although not all, fish populations would recover.

Placing restrictions on specific species of fish, however, does not necessarily solve the problem; it just transfers additional pressure onto other species that aren't protected, jeopardizing their populations. This is a serious concern, because marine ecosystems are so sensitive that overexploitation of *any* species—from shrimp to sharks—will adversely affect other species as well.

Despite overwhelming evidence that fish populations worldwide are in serious decline, we remain incredibly complacent regarding commercial fishing. In order to ensure that Earth's oceans maintain a rich and varied biota in the future, governments must impose, and enforce, sustainable marine harvesting practices now.

Part IV: Saving Civilization

We stand now where two roads diverge... The road we have long been traveling is deceptively easy, a smooth superhighway on which we progress with great speed, but at its end lies disaster. The other fork of the road / the one less traveled by / offers our last, our only chance to reach a destination that assures the preservation of the earth.

—Rachel Carson

13: Increase Awareness

For having lived long, I have experienced many instances of being obliged, by better information or fuller consideration, to change opinions, even on important subjects, which I once thought right but found to be otherwise.

—Benjamin Franklin

LEARNING TO LEARN BETTER

It may seem that we have addressed a number of unrelated issues and problems in this discussion so far, but that is not the case. They are all inextricably linked and have a common cause. All of these problems exist, because the adoption of agriculture set us on a course of artificial development that we are not yet mature enough as a species to manage responsibly. *None of the problems associated with civilization can be solved independently, but all of them can be solved collectively if we simply raise our awareness and act more responsibly.* The first step in this process is to transcend numerous preexisting irrational opinions and beliefs.

TRANSCEND EXISTING DOGMAS

There is an old adage concerning a lost individual who, when asking for directions, is told, "I know where you are trying to go, but you can't get there from here." Obviously, the adage was not intended to be taken literally, but it serves well to illustrate the difficulties that can be encountered when trying to achieve a goal from an inopportune location. That is the dilemma we are faced with today when trying to save civilization.

In order to achieve sustainability, we will have to modify our behavior, and since our behavior is based, to a very large degree, on opinions and beliefs we have indiscriminately assimilated throughout our lives, we need to reevaluate them objectively. Those that can be defended rationally and/or have increased our awareness should be preserved and those that cannot be defended rationally and/or have impaired our awareness should be discarded.

This task will be difficult for a number of reasons. Foremost among them is that we have all been indoctrinated *not* to question the dogmas we have been indoctrinated with—regardless of how improbable they may be. However, maintaining irrational dogmas is not particularly rewarding, and it takes a great deal of effort. Consequently, many people will relish the opportunity to transcend them. Unfortunately, there are others who have been so thoroughly indoctrinated that they may not even be willing to try.

In any event, we cannot achieve sustainability, unless we behave responsibly, and we cannot behave responsibly unless (until), we transcend many of the irrational opinions and beliefs that we have been indoctrinated with.

DISCOURAGE DECEPTION

Increasing general awareness will also require that we discourage the future conveyance of disinformation through deception. This may seem like an impossible task, but conceptually, it is actually quite simple. All we have to do is begin to hold everyone accountable for what they say. This is a reasonable expectation, since our future well-being is dependent, to a large degree, on information we receive abstractly from others.

In fact, there should be social consequences for the dissemination of misinformation and disinformation ranging from loss of respect for minor infractions to complete social ostracism for more serious offenses. This would require that we establish social perspectives that value integrity and reputation above wealth and power.

Currently, in the United States, we tolerate the dissemination of disinformation to achieve desired results, whether it is intended to win elections, gain adherents, be hired for jobs, sell products, or whatever. We regard this as acceptable behavior, because our society maintains highly competitive strategies that reward success at almost any cost.

Our complacency regarding deception is remarkable in light of how much damage it causes. Consider, for example, what happened when former presidents Johnson and Bush deceived us into supporting unnecessary wars (see Chapter 2: Becoming Human, and Chapter 5: Government). If our expectations had been higher regarding the conveyance of information, would they actually have risked their reputations conveying deceptive information? And if our expectations had been higher, would we have believed them? Possibly—but probably not.

These are two extreme examples of what can happen when we become overly tolerant of deception, but deception adversely affects us in lesser ways—many times—every day.

DISCOURAGE INDOCTRINATION

In the future, we will also have to discourage the conveyance of polarizing dogma through indoctrination. In many ways, it is more insidious than disinformation. Deceptions are amendable, but many dogmas are not. They can incite polarity and animosity that lasts for generations.

It is quite likely, for example, that neither Johnson nor Bush would have deceived the American public into fighting wars if they themselves had not already been indoctrinated to fear, distrust, and hate cultures with different political, religious, and economic ideologies.

Indoctrination is one of the most expedient ways to establish solidarity within social groups—which isn't necessarily bad—but the most effective way to establish solidarity through indoctrination is to incite fear and/or hatred of other social groups, whether they are racial, political, religious, cultural, or other. Consequently, although indoctrination helps to establish solidarity *within* social groups, it tends to incite polarity *between* them: conditions that impede inter-societal solidarity, interdependency, and cooperation.

EVALUATE THE CREDIBILITY OF INFORMATION

We can try to discourage the dissemination of disinformation and dogma, but self-serving individuals profit so much from its successful conveyance that they will undoubtedly continue to rely on it. Our best defense against assimilating dogma is to:

- determine the motives for its dissemination, and to

- assess the probability of its content

There are two primary motives for disseminating information:

- to *inform* (through education), and

- to *persuade* (through deception or indoctrination)

While neither motive is necessarily accurate or inaccurate, information that is intended to inform is far more likely to be accurate, or at least credible, than information that is intended to persuade.

When it comes to assessing the probability of information, it is worth considering some advice offered by Buddha:

Believe nothing, no matter where you read it, or who said it,
no matter if I have said it, unless it agrees with your own reason
and your own common sense.

We tend to think of common sense as intuitive, but that is not true. Common sense is actually developed through objective experience (nurture not nature). Unfortunately, individuals who have been deceived or indoctrinated—which is all of us—have correspondingly diminished capacities for exercising common sense.

We are particularly susceptible to deception and indoctrination, because it is our nature to trust people in positions of authority—people who regularly rely on deception and indoctrination to advance their own positions and/or ideologies. This problem is exacerbated by our inclination to share with others what we "learn" from them, perpetuating the deceptions and delusions we have assimilated.

The abstract learning process is flawed, but we long ago committed ourselves to it. We have no choice but to make it work. We can do that, because we are an adaptable species that craves knowledge. This is a bond that connects us all, and if fostered, it can be used to increase our collective awareness and improve our long-term survival prospects.

Sustainability is dependent upon responsible behavior—responsible behavior is dependent upon increasing awareness—and increasing awareness is dependent upon refining the abstract learning process.

14: Recognition

When one tugs at a single thing in nature,
he finds it attached to the rest of the world.

—John Muir

All living organisms compete with each other to survive and reproduce. In a natural state of existence, the playing field is generally pretty level, so no individuals within a species or individual species have profoundly unfair advantages over other individuals or species.

That is no longer true. Artificial development has provided us with grossly unfair advantages over other members of our species and many other species. We tend to regard this advantage as a manifestation of natural selection, but that is not the case. Artificial development has enabled us to *temporarily* circumvent natural selection. That does not mean that we are better or more deserving than other species.

Arguably, no species should have that much power. Certainly, we are not sophisticated enough to manage it responsibly, nor, more alarmingly, are we humble to realize it.

Popular belief maintains that our elevated status as the dominant mammal species on Earth is both deserved and secure. That is not the case at all. The ultimate success or failure of civilization depends, to a large degree, on how responsibly we learn to manage it.

Currently, we are not managing civilization responsibly at all. We are grossly over-consuming Earth's resources, exterminating plant and animal species en masse, and irreparably damaging the environment. Our wanton behavior has raised concerns that we may eventually destroy Earth. That concern is probably unfounded. We are not *that* powerful, but we are certainly powerful enough to destroy Earth's capacity to sustain civilization. In fact, we already have, at least in its present state. Our clever utilization of artificial development has enabled us to forestall the consequences of our transgression, but that can't continue. If we persist on our present course, civilization will collapse.

One of our primary obligations as civilized beings is to minimize the negative impact artificial development has on other species and the environment. If we can manage to incorporate that perspective into our collective awareness and behavior, we may be able to save civilization and pass on to our children, if not a healthy planet, at least one that is beginning to heal from thousands of years of abuse.

Extinct species cannot be brought back, and some of the environmental damage that we have been responsible for cannot be repaired, but we can initiate positive change. For far too long, we have maintained a state of relative *un*awareness regarding the responsibilities intrinsic to civilized existence—the result of which is an accumulation of problems that now threaten our future.

It is essential that we raise our awareness to the degree that we recognize that civilization is in trouble. Unfortunately, many people do not believe that civilization could ever collapse—especially to the degree that it could not be salvaged. This is odd in light of the fact that every major civilized society, even the most powerful empires, *did* collapse: frequently, completely and permanently.

The collapse of societies in the past was undoubtedly very disruptive to those societies—especially the upper classes within them—but they did not severely, adversely affect surrounding societies, because they were not interdependent.

That is no longer the case. Societies are now *completely* interdependent. If a major society collapsed today, it would severely, adversely affect many other societies—perhaps even initiating a chain reaction that would lead to the collapse of civilization.

Almost everyone would be willing to modify their behavior if they believed civilization was at risk of *imminent* collapse—but they don't. That is not because there isn't sufficient evidence—it is all around us. Severe habitat degradation, pollution, climate change, ocean acidification, overpopulation, rampant species extinction, etc., are all indications that civilization is in trouble.

Our inability and/or unwillingness to recognize the risks we are faced with can be compared to the perspectives maintained by the captain, crew, and passengers on *Titanic*. Like the *Titanic*, civilization is traveling at high speed on a course that is fraught with danger—and like *Titanic*, we are receiving warnings and ignoring them—and like *Titanic*, whose captain, crew, and passengers believed that their ship was unsinkable, we believe that civilization is invincible.

But as we all know, the captain, crew, and passengers of *Titanic* were wrong. At 11:40 p.m. on April 14, 1912, *Titanic* struck an iceberg and, within three hours, sank to the bottom of the sea, leaving 1,503 men, women, and children to die in the frigid waters. Unlike *Titanic*, however, civilization hasn't encountered an obstacle large enough to founder it—yet.

However, if we continue on our present course—at our present speed, we inevitably will. The main difference being that when it happens, the entire human race will be affected, not just 2,208 passengers on a ship. The other difference is that there will be no one to rescue the survivors and no place to recover from the disaster.

Nearly everyone agrees that civilization cannot continue on its present course indefinitely, but because most people do not believe that civilization is at risk of *immanent* collapse, they are not willing to modify their behavior sufficiently to alter its course and/or speed. They tend to regard those of us who are concerned, as alarmists.

If they are right, and we alter the course of civilization, the worst that can happen is that we reduce our population, stop driving species to extinction, refrain from over-consuming renewable and nonrenewable resources, and allow the environment to heal—before the last bell rings, so to speak. Conversely, if they are wrong, and we do not alter the course of civilization, it will collapse, perhaps much sooner than expected.

Saving civilization entails far more than reducing carbon emissions, building wind generators, recycling newspapers, and replanting forests. It will require achieving greater awareness and recognizing our responsibilities as civilized beings.

15: Accountability

It is easy to dodge our responsibilities, but we cannot dodge the consequences of dodging our responsibilities.

—Josiah Charles Stamp

Once problems are recognized, the next step is to accept accountability for solving them. Unfortunately, many of the problems that threaten civilization today are complex, imposing, and frequently not directly of our making, so there is great temptation to deny accountability.

Denial is an understandable reaction. However, the problems that threaten civilization today are chronic and need to be addressed *now*. If we refuse or otherwise fail to deal with them, we will be saddling our children with what could easily prove to be an insurmountable accumulation of problems. In civilized states of existence, it is each generation's responsibility to accept accountability for the problems encountered during their tenures—regardless of who created them or how great they may be.

Beyond accepting accountability, we also have to demand it from others. Irresponsible behavior is chronic in modern societies, primarily because we do not hold each other accountable for what we say and do. By not demanding accountability, we are allowing individuals and societies to profit from behavior that adversely affects other individuals, other societies, other species, and the environment.

Greed is certainly the primary motive behind most irresponsible behavior, but ignorance and apathy are others. A great deal of damage is done by people who are just "doing their jobs," "following orders," or "not breaking any rules." These excuses are used by nearly everyone today and are considered socially *semi*-acceptable—arguably, they shouldn't be.

If we support corporations that produce harmful products, we are partly responsible for the damage they create. If we support religions that convey polarizing dogmas, we are partly responsible for the animosity and violence that exists in the world today. If we support governments that invade other countries, we are partially responsible for the murders that are perpetrated there. By demanding greater accountability from *everyone* and *every society*, we can alleviate a great deal of the irresponsible behavior that is so prevalent today.

Solving civilization's problems is every nation's responsibility. However, it is only fair that the United States take the lead in this endeavor. Partly because we are culpable for creating so many of the problems, and partly because we have the wealth, resources, and influence to solve them. We have always regarded ourselves as a world leader; now is the time for us to prove it.

16: Assess Impact

Man has lost the capacity to foresee and forestall. We will end by destroying the earth.

—Albert Schweitzer

Competitive development has enabled *us*, its most successful practitioners, to become the dominant members of the dominant mammal species on Earth—by a substantial margin—in a relatively short period of time. Consequently, *we* understandably regard it as an extremely positive survival strategy. But that perspective is not at all objective. While competitive development is providing us with many short-term survival advantages, it is severely, adversely affecting other members of our species, other species, and the environment—conditions that diminish, rather than enhance, our long-term survival prospects. In other words, we are currently devoted to a survival strategy that is unsustainable.

Establishing a sustainable state of existence will require that we carefully monitor our effects on the environment as objectively as possible and use that information to establish responsible developmental practices.

Objectively assessing the impacts of civilization will be difficult, because there are currently no definitive judgment parameters to rely on. Artificial development is intrinsically a destructive survival strategy. It requires the clearing and claiming of land to grow crops; build storage facilities, permanent housing, fences, roads, dams, irrigation and sanitation systems;

and many other activities that adversely affect natural habitats and displace existing plant and animal species.

Nevertheless, there is assumedly a level at which artificial development can be practiced sustainably. Our responsibility is to figure out where that level is and not exceed it. Ironically, civilization is at risk of collapse today, not because artificial development has proven ineffective, but because it is too effective. Artificial development encourages and enables rampant population growth (see Chapter 3: The Adoption of Agriculture), which means that we have to continuously clear and claim more land to build more storage facilities, more housing, more fences, more roads, more dams, more irrigation and sanitation systems, and on and on—all of which adversely affects more natural habitats and displaces more plant and animal species. When will this destructive cycle end?

It will end when we exhaust Earth's capacity to sustain us, and civilization collapses, or when we mature sufficiently to adopt sustainable developmental practices. The choice is ours.

17: Practice Responsible Agriculture

There is a sufficiency in the world for man's need but not for man's greed.

—Mohandas K. Gandhi

SUSTAINABLE AGRICULTURE

There are very few places on Earth where farmers still practice responsible agriculture. This is primarily because agriculture is now based primarily on greed rather than need. In an attempt to maximize yields and profits, farmers have come to regard soil as simply a medium that holds plants in place, while they are fed chemicals that allow them to grow. This approach enables farmers to reap huge profits, but it depletes soil fertility to the degree that most agricultural land can no longer support crops naturally.

We now rely almost completely on unsustainable agricultural practices to sustain us, and that is a scary thought. In recognition of this disturbing trend, the US government felt compelled in 1990 to define sustainable agriculture in Public Law 101-624, Title XVI, Subtitle A, Section 1683, as:

> an integrated system of plant and animal production practices having a site-specific application that will, over the long-term,

satisfy human food and fiber needs; enhance environmental quality and the natural resource base upon which the agricultural economy depends; make the most efficient use of nonrenewable resources and on-farm resources and integrate, where appropriate, natural biological cycles and controls; sustain the economic viability of farm operations; and enhance the quality of life for farmers and society as a whole.[117]

Unfortunately, there are no legal requirements or even social expectations that farmers adopt sustainable agricultural practices. However, the fact that the US government recognized that the sustainability of agriculture as an important issue may indicate that certain requirements and/or expectations will be implemented sometime in the future.

CURRENT AGRICULTURAL PRACTICES

In order to understand the problems associated with modern agriculture, it is important to realize that agriculture is no longer a service intended to feed people; it is business intended to generate maximum short-term profits—primarily for large corporations.

Beginning in the 1970s, corporations began to buy up small family farms and consolidate them into larger, more "economically efficient" factory farms. At the same time, these corporations began to buy up or merge with related agricultural corporations that produced seed, fertilizers, etc. This strategy is known as *horizontal consolidation*. They also began to buy up or merge with industries devoted to the processing and distribution of agricultural products. This strategy is known as *vertical coordination*. Ostensibly, the motive for horizontal consolidation and vertical coordination is to increase efficiency. But, the actual goal of all such activities is arguably to achieve what is known as *market power*.

---

117 http://www.sustainabletable.org/intro/whatis/

Market power can be achieved when four corporations control 40 percent of any given market. When that occurs, they can control markets and maximize their profits.

Unfortunately, when market power is achieved by agricultural corporations whose motives are solely to maximize short-term profits—chronic long-term problems for our species, other species, and the environment inevitably follow. Our government has been aware of the risks associated with market power in agriculture for a long time, and it has repeatedly tried to prevent it by passing restrictive acts:

- 1916: US Grain Standards Act,

- 1921: Packers and Stockyards Act,

- 1922: Capper-Volstead Act,

- 1930: Perishable Agricultural Commodities Act,

- 1936: Commodity Exchange Act,

- 1967: Agricultural Fair Practices Act, and

- 1999: Livestock Mandatory Price Reporting Act.

Each of these acts was intended, at least in part, to restrict market power in agriculture. Even with all of these protections in place, however, agricultural corporations have managed to establish market power in virtually every segment of the industry—from production to distribution—by substantially more than 40 percent.

Within the production industry, Monsanto, Novartis, Dow Chemical, and DuPont have surfaced as the leaders. They insist they are devoted to sustainable agriculture, but their objectives are primarily to sustain market power—at whatever costs to us, other species, and the environment.

With market power, corporations like Monsanto can regulate the dynamics of agriculture in ways that favor them. They can decide which varieties of which crops are planted by making only those varieties available to growers.

This is what they are attempting to do right now, and they will undoubtedly succeed—if we let them. Allowing giant self-serving corporations like Monsanto to control the future of agriculture is not in anyone's long-term best interests, even their own, but their concerns are not for us or the future—only for themselves and the present.

Unfortunately, we cannot rely on government representatives to solve these problems because they represent the agricultural corporations—not us. Corporations like Monsanto typically contribute to the campaigns of all candidates, so that regardless of who gets elected, they will be beholden to them. This problem can only be alleviated through comprehensive campaign reform (see Chapter 19: Reform Government).

In the meantime, our best approach, although it may seem rather inept, is to refuse to support agricultural corporations by not purchasing their products. This is our power over them. In the long run, consumer power is far more potent than market power.

Agricultural corporations like Monsanto, Novartis, Dow Chemical, and DuPont have committed themselves to an agricultural future utilizing *only* patented, genetically modified seeds owned and distributed by them. Consumers worldwide object to this irresponsible approach and have requested mandatory labeling of products that contain GM crops, so they can be avoided.

Recently, Pamm Larry, a concerned activist from Chico, California, initiated Proposition 37: a bill in California that would have mandated the labeling of products containing GM crops. According to an ABC poll, 52 percent of Americans think GM foods are unsafe, 93 percent think the government should mandate labeling of GM foods, and 57 percent indicated they would avoid buying foods that were labeled as such.[118]

---

118 http://abcnews.go.com/Technology/story?id=97567&page=1#.UJqdWmk-th7

Unfortunately, the bill failed to pass—primarily because Monsanto, DuPont, Syngenta, and other agro-chemical corporations in conjunction with junk-food giants such as Kraft and PepsiCo contributed $46 million to a campaign of deception to defeat it. So far, these corporations have been powerful enough to avoid mandatory labeling, but the will of consumers will eventually prevail.

To thwart irresponsible agricultural practices (such as the use of GM crops) will require international commitment. In that regard, the rest of the world is way ahead of the United States. More than twenty countries have already implemented at least partial bans on the importation or production of GM crops. Additionally, there are now sixty countries that mandate its labeling.

PUBLIC POWER

Monsanto is a huge corporation, but according to their website, there are only eleven members on their board of directors.[119] Remarkably, those eleven individuals are imposing their will over 314 million Americans! How can that happen? A vast minority can impose their will over a vast majority, if they are very committed to achieving a goal and the majority is unaware of their intentions and/or apathetic to them. In this case, the minority is very committed to profit, and the majority is both unaware and apathetic.

Conversely, if people are aware and proactive, they can control even the largest corporations. *Public power is formidable.* As it affects the production and distribution of GM foods, Jeffery Smith, executive director of the Institute for Responsible Technology, in a 2010 interview, stated:

> The concept is that GMOs give no consumer benefits. So, if even a small percentage of consumers were avoiding brands

---

119 http://www.monsanto.com/whoweare/Pages/board-of-directors.aspx

that use GMOs, the companies would switch to non-GMO ingredients in order to maintain their market share. So we think that if just 5% of U.S. shoppers were to avoid GMO ingredients, then this would be sufficient to create a tipping point to knock them out of the market totally.[120]

Stopping the use of GM crops is essential. It is probably already too late to save soybeans and **canola** from permanent GMO contamination, but there is still time to save wheat, potatoes, and possibly corn—if we act now. Toward that end, Pamm Larry suggests that we:[121]

- educate ourselves about GMOs and their "potential" health risks;

- refuse to buy GMO products;

- ask restaurants, grocery stores, etc. whether the foods they serve or sell are GMO-free and how they know that;

- boycott businesses that sell GMO products;

- contact representatives in government to pass laws mandating the labeling of products with GMO crops in them;

- encourage representatives in government to enact legislation prohibiting the patenting of life;

- help fund organizations, individuals, and attorneys who are committed to achieving sustainable agriculture;

- encourage non-GM farmers to sue neighboring GMO farmers when their crops contaminate their own (this would make them less inclined to plant genetically modified crops);

120 http://vitalitymagazine.com/article/feature-interview-on-gmos-helke-ferrie-and-jeffrey-smith/

121 personal communication

- change the way we do business in America; and

- do more!

The Non-GMO Shopping Guide website recommends that we:

- buy certified organic products (certified organic products cannot intentionally contain any GMO products);

- look for Non-GMO Project seals on products;

- avoid at-risk ingredients, such as soybeans, canola, cottonseed, corn, [corn syrup], and sugar from sugar beets; and

- buy products listed in their shopping guide (available online).[122]

SUPPORT ORGANIC AGRICULTURE

In an ideal world, everyone would eat only organically grown foods. Unfortunately, that is not going to happen anytime soon. Yet the closer we can come to achieving that goal, the better off our species, other species, and the environment will be. Fortunately, there are increasing numbers of growers and consumers who are aware of this and are working diligently to promote the organic food movement.

Until very recently, all agricultural crops were organically grown. It wasn't until the advent of chemical fertilizers in the early 1900s and herbicides and pesticides in the early 1950s that farmers began to practice nonorganic agriculture. This does not mean organic agriculture is necessarily sustainable, but it is at least *potentially* sustainable, whereas nonorganic agriculture is definitely not.

---

122 http://action.responsibletechnology.org/p/salsa/web/common/public/signup?signup_
    page_KEY=7042

In 1990, the Organic Food Production Act was passed, requiring the USDA to develop national standards for organic products. The USDA defines organic food as food produced by farmers:

> who emphasize the use of renewable resources and the conservation of soil and water to enhance environmental quality for future generations. Organic meat, poultry, eggs, and dairy products come from animals that are given no antibiotics or growth hormones. Organic food is produced without using most conventional pesticides; fertilizers made with synthetic ingredients or sewage sludge; bioengineering; or ionizing radiation.

According to the Rodale Institute website, organic farms in the United States on average were:

> more profitable than the average of all farms in the U.S., according to results of the first-ever federal census of organic agriculture. A total of 14,540 organic farms had sales of $21.1 billion from more than four million acres of farm and rangeland.[123]

Consequently, organic agriculture now accounts for about 10 percent of agricultural revenue (not product) in the United States. This is an indication that a significant number of Americans are aware of what is going on in the food industry and are willing to seek out and pay more for organic products. However, agricultural corporations have been quick to exploit consumer concerns. Many of them have purchased respected suppliers of organic products so that they can exploit their trusted names, and all of them are now marketing products labeled as "natural." Unfortunately, "natural" products can contain toxic chemical pesticides and herbicides, genetically modified organisms, antibiotics, and growth hormones; they

---

123 http://www.rodaleinstitute.org/20100319/nf_USDA-census-shows-profitability-of-organic-farming

can be grown in sludge and irradiated to help preserve them; and they do not have to consider the welfare of animals, environmental pollution, or agricultural sustainability during their production. In other words, the designation *natural* on food products means absolutely nothing.[124] Don't be fooled by it.

Responsible agricultural *is* organic agriculture, and its adoption is a critical step in the pursuit of sustainability and the future of civilization. So much so that everyone should involve themselves in supporting it in whatever way they can.

---

124 http://www.stonyfield.com/why-organic/organic-vs-natural

18: Adopt Responsible Diets

*Nothing will benefit human health and increase chances
for survival of life on Earth as much as the evolution to a
vegetarian diet.*

—Albert Einstein

Surprisingly, one of the most effective ways to take pressure off Earth's
biota and the environment is to revert back to a primarily plant-based diet.
Raising livestock has many unexpected negative effects on both.

AIR

According to the UN News Center website published in 2006, raising cattle generates more greenhouse gas pollution (as measured in CO2
equivalency) than all of the cars, trucks, trains, ships, and planes together.
Henning Steinfeld, senior UN Food and Agriculture Organization (FAO)
official, stated, "Livestock are one of the most significant contributors to
today's most serious environmental problems."

Livestock are currently responsible for about 9 percent of the carbon
dioxide introduced into the atmosphere from human-related activities.
Additionally, livestock generates 65 percent of human-related nitrous oxide
(which holds 296 times more heat than carbon dioxide), 37 percent of all

human-induced methane (which holds 23 times more heat than carbon dioxide), and 64 percent of the ammonia (which contributes significantly to acid rain).

Unfortunately, as people become more affluent, they consume more meat and dairy products. Global meat production is projected to increase from 229 million tons in 1999/2001 to 465 million tons in 2050, and the global milk output is expected to increase from 580 million tons to 1,043 million tons.

There is no getting around the fact that raising livestock has disastrous effects on Earth's atmosphere.

WATER

CONSUMPTION

Another concern regarding livestock is water usage. In the United States, more than half of all the water used (not just for agriculture) is devoted to livestock production. Most agricultural activities require lots of water.

Statistics vary regarding livestock use of water, but a recent study at the University of Twente, in the Netherlands, determined that it takes about 1,800 gallons of water to produce one pound of beef.[125] They also determined that it takes about 20 times more water to produce a calorie from animal sources than plant sources. This inefficient use of Earth's limited water resources is very destructive to the environment and extremely shortsighted. In most agricultural regions, water must be diverted from somewhere else or pumped from "fossil" aquifers to supply it.

On the High Plains of North America, for example, crops are irrigated with water taken from the Ogallala Aquifer. It is regarded as a "fossil" aquifer, because it was created about ten million years ago during the Pliocene epoch and is recharged solely from rainwater and snowmelt. Because the

---

125 http://phys.org/news/2011-01-footprints-animal-proteins.html

High Plains are semiarid, the recharge rate is very slow—on average, about one inch annually. Unfortunately, the Ogallala aquifer is being depleted at the rate of about 2.7 feet per year. Consequently, if withdrawals continue at the present rate, it could be effectively depleted sometime during the first half of the twenty-first century.[126]

The Ogallala Aquifer is an incredibly valuable resource to this country, but we are allowing it to be exploited irresponsibly. Why? Because the dynamics of our free market economy allow for personal ownership of such resources, which allows individuals the right to overly exploit them if they choose.

In the United States, agriculture accounts for about 87 percent of fresh water consumed each year. Livestock only consume about 1.3 percent of that amount directly. However, when forage and grain are factored in, that amount rises to about 50 percent.[127]

According to the USDA Economic Research Service, Americans consume about 25 billion pounds of beef each year.[128] Raising that much beef requires about 45 trillion gallons of water—20 times more than the 2.25 trillion gallons that would have been required to produce the same amount of calories from plant sources.

Raising livestock for human consumption is an incredibly inefficient use of Earth's limited water resources.

POLLUTION

Raising livestock also contributes profoundly to water pollution: directly (from animal waste, antibiotics, and hormones) as well as indirectly (from the use of chemical fertilizers, herbicides, and pesticides used on crops to feed livestock).[129]

---

126 http://www.waterencyclopedia.com/Oc-Po/Ogallala-Aquifer.html

127 http://www.news.cornell.edu/releases/aug97/livestock.hrs.html

128 http://www.ers.usda.gov/topics/animal-products/cattle-beef/statistics-information.
    aspx#.UbjXWxYx78s

129 http://www.un.org/apps/news/story.asp?newsID=20772&CR1=warning

We already addressed the issue of chemical pollution in Chapter 11, so here we will deal specifically with pollution from animal waste. The USDA estimates that around five hundred million tons of manure is produced annually by livestock and poultry. That is more than three times the EPA estimate of 150 million tons of human waste produced each year. And in comparison to the lesser amount of human waste, the management and disposal of animal waste is poorly regulated.[130]

According to the National Resource Defense Council (NRDC), livestock waste is usually stored in large open-air lagoons—that are prone to leaks and spills—which adversely affect Earth's biota. The following is a list of some examples:

- In 1995, an eight-acre hog waste lagoon in North Carolina burst, spilling twenty-five million gallons of manure into the New River. The spill killed about ten million fish and closed 364,000 acres of coastal wetlands to shell fishing.

- From 1995 to 1998, a total of one thousand spills or pollution incidents occurred at livestock feedlots in ten states, and two hundred manure-related fish kills resulted in the death of thirteen million fish.

- When Hurricane Floyd hit North Carolina in 1999, at least five manure lagoons burst, and approximately forty-seven lagoons were completely flooded.

- Runoff of chicken and hog waste from factory farms in Maryland and North Carolina is believed to have contributed to outbreaks of Pfiesteria piscicida, killing millions of fish.

- Nutrients in animal waste cause algal blooms, which use up oxygen in the water (see Chapter 11: Pollution). Animal waste

---

130 http://www.theenvironmentalblog.org/2008/05/farm-animal-waste-an-
    environmental-hazard/

in the Mississippi River created a seven thousand-square mile to eight-thousand-square-mile "dead zone" in the Gulf of Mexico, where there is not enough oxygen to support aquatic life.

- Ammonia, a toxic form of nitrogen released in gas form during waste disposal, can be carried more than three hundred miles through the air before being dumped back onto the ground or into the water, where it causes algal blooms and fish kills.[131]

Raising livestock is a primary contributor to water pollution in the United States and other livestock-producing countries.

LAND

Currently, 30 percent of Earth's entire land surface is devoted to livestock production. About 30 percent of that land is pasture not suitable for raising crops, but 33 percent of Earth's arable land is now devoted to producing feed for livestock. If the projected figures cited earlier are correct, 60 percent of Earth's entire land surface will be devoted to raising livestock by 2050, and 66 percent of Earth's arable land will be devoted to producing feed for livestock.

The increasing allocation of land for livestock use is exacerbated by the fact that unsound grazing practices have already degraded 20 percent of Earth's pastureland. According to David Pimentel, professor of ecology and agriculture at Cornell University's College of Agriculture and Life Sciences:

> Livestock are directly or indirectly responsible for much of the soil erosion in the United States. On lands where feed grain is produced, soil loss averages 5.2 tons per acre per year. Pasture lands are eroding at a slower pace, at an average of 2.4 tons

---

131 http://www.nrdc.org/water/pollution/ffarms.asp

per acre per year. But erosion may exceed 40 tons on severely overgrazed pastures, and 54 percent of U.S. pasture land is being overgrazed.[132]

This is not just a problem in the United States. Pastureland degradation is taking place everywhere on Earth. It is a worldwide problem that needs to be addressed now. And there is only one way to do that—by reducing our dependency on livestock. This will require that we change our diets and lower our population.

BIOTA

FORESTS

Another major concern regarding livestock production is deforestation. The Massachusetts Institute of Technology (MIT) recently studied the correlation between rain forest loss and beef production. They determined that for every burger we eat, about fifty-five square feet of rain forest is cleared. Many fast-food chains today claim they do not use rain forest beef, but the USDA doesn't have an adequate system for labeling where beef comes from, so beef grown in rain forests regularly passes through processing plants in the United States and is sold as domestic meat.[133]

Consequently, if we eat beef, we are contributing to the loss of rain forests—whether we like it or not. In any event, regardless of where rain forest beef is sold, approximately one acre of rain forest is cleared every eight seconds to raise more beef. The only way we can stop the destruction of Earth's remaining rain forests is, once again, is to reduce our dependency on livestock by changing our diets and lowering our population.

---

132 http://www.news.cornell.edu/releases/aug97/livestock.hrs.html

133 http://www.examiner.com/article/brazil-says-us-to-blame-for-rainforest-deforestation

MARINE FISHERIES

For health reasons, many Americans have recently decided to eat less red meat and more fish. Due to increasing chemical pollution in Earth's oceans, that may not be a wise decision. Nevertheless, increased reliance on marine fisheries is no longer an option. We have depleted most species of harvestable fish to the degree that even when utilizing the most aggressive harvesting strategies, harvests are declining each year.

Consequently, we will not be able to rely on more fish in the future; we will not even be able to rely on the same amount of fish presently being harvested. In fact, if we do not voluntarily, significantly reduce fish harvests, there will be no fish to harvest in the future.

There is only one responsible way to deal with this situation. Governments need to place severe restrictions on almost all fish harvests and moratoriums on others—now. We also need to reduce carbon emissions to avoid further ocean acidification—now. If we implement these changes and fish populations recover, then sustainable harvest levels can be established.

In the mean time, we will have to rely much less on marine fisheries. Transferring that reliance to farmed fish, chickens, and pigs may seem like the obvious solution, but it is not. Each of these industries relies very heavily on marine harvests to feed its stock. Currently, thirty million tons (36 percent) of the world's annual fisheries' catch is ground up and fed to farmed fish, chickens, and pigs.[134] Consequently, their availability will probably diminish in the future as well.

Like it or not, we will have to rely much more heavily on plant-based diets in the future. Additionally, one again, solutions to our problems necessitate comprehensive population reduction.

---

134 http://news.mongabay.com/2009/1118-hance_fishmeal.html#

PLANT VERSUS ANIMAL PROTEIN

Reducing animal protein from our diets would have a greater positive impact on Earth's biota and the environment than: supporting alternative energy sources, driving energy-efficient vehicles, purchasing low-wattage light bulbs, switching to low-flush toilets, using biodegradable cleaning products, recycling, and all of the other popular green activities currently in use today. It would also be better for us.

We have been taught that we need to consume lots of meat and dairy products to obtain enough protein and calcium to stay healthy. That is not true. For the vast majority of hominid existence, we were vegan—as are most of our closest relatives. Sufficient protein and calcium are easily obtained from plant-based diets.

It is unlikely, though, that our species would have advanced as far as it has if we had remained vegan. Adopting omnivorous diets enabled our ancestors to migrate out of central Africa into temperate regions, while our vegan relatives were forced to remain where they were. Consequently, our reliance on animal protein has served us very well.

Nevertheless, eating meat is a relatively recent adaptation for our species. Our bodies can process animal products reasonably well, but our metabolisms evolved over millions of years to process plants, not animals. We have the long digestive tracts of herbivores not carnivores. We also have livers that produce levels of cholesterol when we consume animal products that kill us more frequently than any other cause. These are ample indications that we do not need—and over the long-term do not tolerate well—animal products.

Until quite recently however, it would have been impractical and unhealthy for those of us who live in temperate climates to maintain vegan diets. Sufficient produce was not available. That is no longer the case. Artificial development provides us with access to healthy, fresh produce year-round. Consequently, we no longer need to rely on animal products to sustain us.

The primary reason we believe we need to consume meat and dairy products to stay healthy is because the FDA and the USDA serve as pimps for the meat and dairy industries, promoting their products.

A continued, or increasing, reliance on animal protein is a choice—not a necessity. According to David Pimentel, professor of ecology and agriculture at Cornell University:

> Each year an estimated 41 million tons of plant protein is fed to U.S. livestock to produce an estimated 7 million tons of animal protein for human consumption. About 26 million tons of the livestock feed comes from grains and 15 million tons from forage crops. For every pound of high-quality animal protein produced, livestock are fed nearly six pounds of plant protein.[135]

Consequently, we do not need animal protein to survive. In fact, we would have access to far more protein if we did not raise livestock. The true cost of raising livestock is not its cost per pound, but its cost to Earth's biota and environment, and that cost is too great to bear.

BOTTLED WATER

Another important step we can all take to mitigate our negative impact on other species and the environment is to stop buying water in plastic bottles. Listed below are some disturbing statistics compiled by the Environmental Working Group regarding bottled water:[136]

- Every twenty-seven hours, Americans consume enough bottled water to circle the entire equator with plastic bottles stacked end-to-end.

---

135 http://www.news.cornell.edu/releases/aug97/livestock.hrs.html

136 http://www.ewg.org/bottled-water-2011-how-much-do-we-drink

- In just a single week, those bottles would stretch more than halfway to the Moon—155,400 miles.

- Between 2004 and 2009, US consumption of bottled water increased by 24 percent. Bottled water sales have more than quadrupled in the last twenty years (BMC 2010).

- The federal government does not mandate that bottled water be any safer than tap water—the chemical pollution standards are nearly identical (EWG 2008). In fact, bottled water is less regulated than tap water.

- Close to half of all bottled water is sourced from municipal tap water (BMC 2010, Food and Water Watch 2010).

- It takes an estimated two thousand times more energy to produce bottled water than to produce an equivalent amount of tap water (Gleick 2009).

- Bottled water production and transportation for the US market consumes more than thirty million barrels of oil each year and produces as much carbon dioxide as two million cars (Gleick 2009).

- Plastic water bottles are the fastest-growing form of municipal solid waste in the United States. Each year, more than four billion pounds of PET plastic bottles end up in landfills or as roadside litter (Corporate Accountability International 2010).

- While plastic bottles can be recycled, most are not. Moreover, plastic never actually degrades; it just breaks down into smaller and smaller pieces. In some parts of the ocean, plastic outweighs plankton by a 6:1 ratio (Moore 2001).

- Bottled water has indirect economic costs. Disposing of plastic water bottle waste, for example, costs cities nationwide an estimated $70 million in landfill tipping fees each year (Corporate Accountability International 2010).

The three major producers of bottled water are Nestle, Coca-Cola, and PepsiCo. They avoid having to comply with federal regulations regarding water quality by bottling *local, sometimes municipal,* water and selling it within that state's border for between 240 and 10,000 times more than the cost of municipal water (which is highly regulated). We have been deceived through clever advertising campaigns to believe bottled water is pure and good for us, and that municipal water is not. According to the NRDC, however, that is not the case. In one test, 33 percent of bottled water tested from different manufacturers contained chemical or bacterial contaminants exceeding those allowed under state and industry standards.[137]

We can all do ourselves and the planet a favor by making greater use of municipal water. Much of it comes out of the tap tasting like chlorine, but chlorine can be filtered out easily with home water-filtering systems—at a fraction of the cost to us and the environment of purchasing bottled water. Reusable plastic bottles or, better yet, small stainless steel thermoses (which also keep the water cool) can be used just as easily to transport it.

Boycotting bottled water is easy. The loss of convenience is minor, and the net positive effects to all species and the environment would be extremely positive.

---

137 http://www.nrdc.org/water/drinking/bw/exesum.asp

19: Reform Government

It is horrifying that we have to fight our own government to save the environment.

—Ansel Adams

A primary responsibility of all societies is to establish some form of government that represents them wisely and equitably. Societies have experimented endlessly with different forms of governments hoping to find one that was consistently reliable, but none have succeeded. Every form of government has experienced both successes and failures, just as they have produced both great and terrible leaders. If there was one form of government that was superior to all others, most societies would have adopted it by now.

In the United States, our founding fathers chose to adopt a republic. As regards it, at the close of the Constitutional Convention in 1787, a woman bystander asked Benjamin Franklin, "Well Doctor, what have we got: a republic or a monarchy?" "A republic," replied Franklin, "if you can keep it."

Franklin's concerns regarding our ability to maintain a republic were well founded. After just over two hundred years, we have allowed special interests to usurp it and replace it with a *corporatocracy*.

Politicians today may wear American flag pins on their lapels and wax patriotic when speaking in public, but those are ploys. Virtually, every one of them owes his or her allegiance directly or indirectly to corporations that sponsored them. Their primary allegiances will necessarily be to them—not to us and not to our country.

CHOOSE RELIABLE LEADERS

In a 2010 nationwide Gallup Poll survey conducted on public trust, only 9 percent of 1,037 Americans polled thought members of Congress could be trusted. That is an appallingly low number, but one that is probably justified. It reflects just how badly we are being represented. It also indicates that Americans are not as ignorant and naive as our leaders seem to think we are.

Unfortunately, in our present corporatocracy we are seldom given the opportunity to vote for candidates who are free to represent us. Instead we are usually forced to vote for the "least-worst" candidates. This is an untenable situation and one that has to be resolved.

CAMPAIGN REFORM

The purpose of elections is to choose reliable leaders who will represent members of societies wisely and equitably. To accomplish that goal requires impartiality in selecting candidates. To insure impartiality in most societies (including our own) will require comprehensive campaign reform, including:

- providing all legitimate candidates with *equal public funds* to run their campaigns;

- providing all legitimate candidates with equal television and radio exposure through objective interviews and debates;

- disallowing private contributions to specific candidates;

- disallowing the use of private funds to run campaigns;

- disallowing campaign advertisements, and most of all:

- eliminating the party political system.

No one who truly believes in democracy could find fault with this approach. It is fair, impartial, and provides a level playing field for all candidates. No potentially worthy candidate could be excluded from consideration, no candidate would have an unfair advantage over other candidates, and each candidate would be free to represent his or her society equitably if elected. Additionally, the public would be much better informed regarding the qualifications of the candidates.

Using public funds to finance campaigns may seem like an exorbitant burden on taxpayers, but the cost of letting special interests control the outcomes of elections is *much* greater to societies over the long run. *Electing representatives should never be regarded as a free market enterprise.*

Unfortunately, initiating campaign reform will be difficult, because special interests will fight vehemently to maintain the status quo. It is, after all, a system that benefits them enormously. The good news regarding election reform, however, is that from a conceptual perspective, implementing it is actually quite simple and relatively inexpensive.

In any event, no matter how we choose our leaders, it is our responsibility to ensure that they represent our long-term best interests, not those of political parties, corporations, religions, or other special interests. Every federal employee—whether elected or appointed, from presidents to members of congress, to judges, to law enforcement personnel—must be made to realize that they are, after all, *public* servants.

20: Regulate Business

*I define globalization as the freedom of our corporations to
invest where and when we want, to produce what we want,
to buy and sell where we want, and to keep all the restrictions
through labor law or other political regulations as slight as
possible.*

—Percy Barnevik (VIP of the Foundation Board of the World
Economic Forum)

EVALUATE ECONOMIC STRATEGIES

Societies generally employ one of two basic economic strategies: socialism
or capitalism. Socialism is undoubtedly an extension of the communal,
egalitarian, social practices employed by primitive foraging societies. It is
based on the assumption that the general welfare of everyone *in* societies is
essential to the general welfare *of* societies. From a social and environmental perspective, socialism is by far the more responsible economic strategy.
However, because it is based on cooperation rather than competition, it is
less dynamic than, and cannot compete with, capitalism.

Conversely, capitalism almost certainly evolved out of our age-old
instinct to hoard as much food as possible to survive winter seasons in temperate climates (see Chapter 2: Becoming Human). In our present artificial
state of existence that impulse has evolved into a truly dynamic economic

strategy, but one that inevitably, adversely affects other members of our species, other species, and the environment—conditions that are not at all conducive to the attainment of sustainable existence.

Consequently, we have a dilemma. We have been indoctrinated to believe that we must choose between socialism (an economic strategy that could sustain us over the long-term, but can't compete with capitalism over the short-term) and capitalism (which can outcompete socialism over the short-term, but cannot sustain us over the long-term). Neither can be relied upon *exclusively* to serve us in the future, but depending upon our backgrounds, most of us have been indoctrinated to regard one or the other of them as an ideology worth fighting and dying for.

ADOPT RESPONSIBLE ECONOMIC STRATEGIES

Many societies in the past have recognized the drawbacks of capitalism and opted to embrace socialism, but none of them succeeded—probably, primarily because they could not compete with capitalist societies.

Capitalist societies have always regarded the failures of socialist societies as evidence that capitalism is superior to socialism, but that is a misconception. *Capitalism can outcompete socialism, but that does not mean that it is superior; only that it is more competitive—which is not the same at all.*

Fiscal conservatives in capitalist societies strive for free market economies, claiming that government intervention impedes fiscal growth. If businesses were always aware of the negative impacts their activities had on people, other societies, other species, and the environment—and conscientious enough to refrain from adversely impacting them, free market economies would work well. Unfortunately, their motives are to generate profit for share holders—not to consider the welfare of people, other societies, other species, or the environment. Consequently, although free market economies can be fiscally very productive, they are inherently, socially and environmentally, very destructive.

If our government had not imposed regulations on business in the past, for example, most of us would be working 12 hour days—seven days a week—in unsafe conditions—with no benefits. We would also still be fogging playgrounds with DDT—destroying the ozone layer with CFC's—and poisoning ourselves (and everyone else) with leaded gasoline.

Government intervention can be horribly oppressive, but big business has demonstrated over and over again that it cannot be trusted to behave responsibly. It cannot even be trusted to manage itself. In the 1980s President Ronald Reagan (a fiscal conservative) initiated a program of banking deregulation to encourage lending and growth. It achieved its desired goal. However, deregulation enabled banks to make extremely irresponsible loans and investments that led, in 2007, to the near collapse of not only the US financial infrastructure, but the rest world's as well.

Whatever economic strategies societies choose to employ in the future, they should incorporate positive aspects of capitalism—such as rewarding personal achievement and contribution. They should also incorporate positive aspects of socialism, such encouraging intra- and inter-societal interdependency and cooperation.

Unlike capitalism and socialism, however, they should also consider the welfare of people, other societies, other species, and the environment. In other words, they should be responsible and sustainable—which means that it will have to be regulated.

In the end, it doesn't really matter whether societies choose to reform socialism or capitalism to achieve these goals. If the economic strategies they develop are realistic and socially and environmentally responsible, they will inevitably end up being very similar.

21: Transcend Religion

A wise man is one who finally realizes that there are some questions one can ask which may have no answers.

—Anon

EVALUATE THE MERITS OF RELIGIONS

Discussing the transcendence of religion is bound to disturb some readers. Unfortunately, that can't be helped. Ideological religious dogma is the source of much of the polarity, animosity, and conflict that exists today. Any attempt to save civilization and achieve sustainability that didn't address the transcendence of religion would be craven and inept.

There are many thousands of religions in the world, but once again we will focus on the Abrahamic religions: Judaism, Christianity, and Islam—because they are currently the most influential and confrontational religions.

As discussed in Chapter 7, each of these religions is based on texts that their adherents claim were given to them directly or indirectly by God. If any of these religions is in possession of such a text, arguably, it would be divine and should be adhered to by everyone.

When evaluating the merits of the Abrahamic religions, we need to determine if Jews, Christians, or Muslims are in possession of a divine text. In order to do that we have to assess the premise of these texts objectively.

If God does exist and did provide religious directives outlining the laws by which he expected people to live by (assuming that he didn't change his mind over time—and wasn't overly perverse), the content of those texts would assumedly be essentially the same. They are not. From this simple realization we can logically conclude that at least two of the texts are not what they are purported to be and are therefore not divine. But which ones?

This is a very contentious issue. Jews, Christians, and Muslims have been killing each other en masse since the inceptions of their religions—striving to assert the legitimacy of their texts. Incredibly, they do this with complete conviction that they are acting with God's approval. This is truly remarkable since Jews, Christians, and Muslims all worship the same god, embrace most of the same prophets and angels, and recognize the historicity (but not necessarily the accuracy of) the biblical events initially related in the Jewish Torah.

Because all of these religions are based on events related in the Torah, the best way to assess their merits is to objectively evaluate those events. If they prove to be historically accurate and plausible, then the possibility that one of the texts is divine should be considered further. If they do not, then all of the texts can be dismissed as fraudulent, because all of them were established based on the historicity of those events.

A number of implausibility issues were addressed in chapter 7. However, it is worth examining one more here to demonstrate just how improbable events related in the Torah can be.

In Numbers: 26 Moses allegedly determined that there were 601,730 fighting age men within eleven of the twelve tribes of Israel (the clans of Levi were not counted because they were assigned priestly duties).

Extrapolating from that number, researchers have calculated that there would have been approximately three million Jews involved in the Exodus from Egypt. Supporting that many people and their stock in the desert for forty years would have been physically impossible. In fact, any attempt to explain how it could have been accomplished would necessarily be absurd.

Absurd explanations occur throughout the Torah. For example, in Numbers: 20:11, while traveling through the Wilderness of Zin on their way to Canaan, Moses allegedly brought forth water from a rock by striking it with his staff. Aside from the fact that such an act is completely implausible, watering that many people from a single spring is not possible. To put the problem in perspective, if each Israelite spent ten seconds quenching his or her thirst, the last person in line would have to wait 347 days for his or her turn to drink. And that schedule doesn't even consider watering the livestock that was traveling with them.

It is also pertinent to note that there is virtually no archaeological evidence to suggest that a large group of Israelites, or anyone else, lived in the Sinai desert at that, or any other time.

When events related in the Torah are evaluated objectively, it becomes abundantly clear that most of them are historically inaccurate—extremely implausible—or both. Logically, this means that the events related in the Torah did not happen and that Torah is not the word of God, and therefore, not divine. It also means, by extension, that neither the Christian Holy Bible nor the Muslim Quran, which are based on the historicity of the events in the Torah are divine texts either.

Accepting religious divinity presents serious challenges for objective adherents of these faiths. There have been more copies of the Holy Bible (which contains the Torah in the Old Testament) and the Quran printed and distributed than any other book—by a substantial number, and yet very few people have actually read them *in their entireties*. This is an extraordinary realization. One would logically assume that everyone would want to read books allegedly authored by God. Actually, many people do try to read them, but can't finish them. Arguably, they find them so implausible that the only way they can maintain faith in them (and their religions) is *not* to read them.

If God does exist and was capable of creating the universe in six days, surely he would have devised a better method for instructing humankind than by providing us with a text or texts relating historically inaccurate and/or implausible events that would be misinterpreted and contested by nearly everyone.

All of the available evidence suggests that the Tanakh, the Holy Bible, and the Quran were composed by unsophisticated individuals who maintained gross misconceptions and prejudices intrinsic to humankind—not by God.

TRANSCEND RELIGIONS

Religion's claim to be mediators between people and God. But that claim cannot be substantiated and is extremely unlikely. They also claim to be instrumental in promoting moral behavior. That claim is completely false. In attempting to assert themselves, religions intentionally incite interreligious polarity that inevitably leads to wide-scale violence including murder. Consequently, contrary to popular belief, the net impact of religions on humanity is decidedly negative.

There are positive aspects of religions that are worth preserving. Unfortunately, because they were originally promoted as divine and inviolate, they have to be accepted or rejected as they are. They cannot be modified.

We have all been indoctrinated to believe that we need religion, but that is not true either. Religion is not a vital, tangible requirement like air, water, food, etc. It is an artificial manifestation of human imagination. If we cease to believe in it, it ceases to exist. The perpetuation of religion is actually dependent upon public *un*awareness.

People who have been exposed to intense religious indoctrination throughout their lives will understandably be reluctant to transcend, or even question their religion's dogmas. However, trying to maintain faith in irrational dogmas is difficult and can be extremely disillusioning. Consequently, many people will relish the opportunity to transcend them. Fortunately, as we become more aware in the future, we will be less susceptible to the dissemination of dogmas and more inclined to reject them.

Everyone has the right to believe what he or she chooses, but almost everyone today is indoctrinated to believe and support a specific religion long before they are mature enough to make objective decisions regarding them. This is unfortunate because religious faith is *not* knowledge or awareness and maintaining it leads inevitably to confusion, delusion, and polarity—hardly conditions that encourage responsible behavior and the attainment of sustainable existence.

GODS AND GODDESSES

Religions have promoted the concept of gods and goddesses so well that 86 percent of the world's population now believes in them—*even though there is no evidence to prove that they exist.*

Those who have been indoctrinated to believe in gods and goddesses have also generally been indoctrinated to regard non-believers as evil or uncaring. That is unfortunate because non-believers are frequently the most aware and conscientious individuals in societies. The 14 percent of the population that does not believe in them is definitely a minority, but it is pertinent to note that they represent the largest *unsolicited* perspective in existence. No one has to be indoctrinated *not* to believe in gods and goddesses. They are simply individuals who choose to base their perspectives on knowledge accumulated through education rather than dogmas accumulated through indoctrination.

Throughout history, and assumedly throughout much of prehistory, people deified and worshipped inanimate celestial bodies, such as the sun, the moon, Mars, Venus, various constellations, etc. They prayed to them and believed their prayers were heard and answered. Today, we know with absolute certainty that none of those entities were actually gods or goddesses, and that none of them heard or answered prayers. We tend to regard those earlier beliefs as quaint and naive, but are our modern beliefs in God any more plausible? Does God actually exist? If so, does he really hear and answer prayers? Or are modern beliefs just as naive?

If anyone tried to prove the existence of God in an objective court of law, the case would probably be dismissed for reason of insufficient evidence. All that we know for certain regarding the creation of the universe is that some force did create it. With that simple explanation, we must be content, because it is currently all that we know. Of one thing we can be fairly certain. God did not create man in *His* image; man created God in *his* image.

22: Encourage Responsible Behavior

*When plunder becomes a way of life for a group of men
living together in society, they create for themselves in the
course of time a legal system that authorizes it and a moral
code that justifies it.*

—Frederic Bastiat

We like to think that moral, responsible behavior is determined by laws that we establish, but that is not quite true. Law, in its purest intention, is the codification of innate *sub*conscious, conscientious behavior into conscious rules and regulations.

Laws are absolutely necessary in artificial societies, but self-serving interests within societies seek to establish laws that allow, encourage, and even mandate, irresponsible, *un*conscionable behavior. Consequently, we are frequently faced with having to choose between behaving conscientiously or adhering to *un*conscionable laws.

Idyllically, social laws would reflect conscience. But we live in highly competitive, irresponsible, artificial societies where conscience gets in the way of what we want. If we adhered solely to conscience, we would not:

- invade other people's countries to take their land and/or exploit their resources;

- overharvest Earth's lands, forests, oceans, lakes, and rivers;

- pollute Earth's lands, forests, oceans, lakes, rivers, and atmosphere;

- allow our population to increase to the determent of other members of our species and other species;

- adopt unsound agricultural practices;

- develop, work for, or invest in, destructive corporations, and on and on.

In other words, we wouldn't do many of the things that have made us— well—great. This is a sobering realization. Is the successful application of artificial development actually dependent upon unconscionable behavior? No, it is not. It just means that we are not as great as we think we are—not even close.

In any event, our goal should be to achieve sustainability, not greatness. In order to do that, we will have to behave much more responsibly than we presently do, and that will require that we behave much more conscientiously than we presently do.

Establishing responsible, conscientious behavior will be difficult. It will necessarily fall on the strongest, most aware, and secure individuals, corporations, governments, and societies to initiate it. Once it is initiated, however, others will undoubtedly follow. The vast majority of humankind is born with conscience, and it is our instinct to adhere to it.

If we strip all of the irrational religious, political, and cultural dogma away from our perspectives, no matter where we are from, our behavior will be remarkably similar, because it is directed by conscience, which is common to all of us.

23: Extend Social Allegiances

The greater the loyalty of a group toward the group, the greater is the motivation among the members to achieve the goals of the group, and the greater the probability that the group will achieve its goals.

—Rensis Likert

For the vast majority of human existence, our survival depended upon our abilities to outcompete non-familial members of our species. Once we adopted agriculture that began to change. The dynamics of artificial development demanded increasing levels of non-familial allegiance and cooperation. The more interdependent we became, the more cooperative we had to be.

It is generally not recognized as such, but the extension of social allegiance is one of our species most remarkable accomplishments. We have progressed a long way in that regard, but we still have a long way to go. Once we crossed the threshold between natural and artificial existence, we inadvertently committed ourselves to achieving comprehensive intra and inter-societal allegiance and cooperation.

INTERDEPENDENCY, ALLEGIANCE, AND COOPERATION

Interdependency, allegiance, and cooperation have increased dramatically over the last twelve thousand years. Socially, we have progressed from living in extended families, to villages, to states, to nations, and finally to international coalitions. The logical next step in this progression is for international coalitions to recognize their interdependency and establish comprehensive international allegiance.

It is imperative that we take this next step. We cannot achieve sustainability unless/until we do. Unfortunately, many societies are convinced that their survival depends on competition. Since they achieved their status through competition, that perspective is understandable. However it is important to realize that virtually *every* major society in the past that relied on competition to sustain itself, eventually collapsed. We do not actually know that sustainability can be achieved through cooperation, because we have never tried it. However, we know for a fact that sustainability cannot be achieved through competition.

Whether increased inter-societal interdependency, allegiance, and cooperation prove positive or negative to our species over the long-term will depend, to a large degree, on how well we learn to integrate them into our survival strategies.

There is a fundamental misunderstanding regarding international interdependency. Affluent societies, like the United States, are becoming more and more dependent on third world countries to provide them with products and services. Some of this interchange represents positive international interdependency and cooperation, but a great deal of it is just abject exploitation. Workers in exporting nations are frequently coerced by corporations to work in substandard conditions—for substandard wages—to produce low-priced products—that can be sold for huge profits by US corporations.

Unfortunately until attitudes change and/or governments intervene to ensure that the exchange is equitable, business interests will inevitably exploit third world countries. Most people, though, if given the opportunity, would willingly choose to support interdependent, cooperative, sustainable relationships with other societies.

RECOGNIZE INTERNATIONAL HOLIDAYS

One of the simplest ways to establish international solidarity might be to recognize and celebrate common holidays. This would be relatively easy because they already exist:

- the spring equinox (March 21)

- the summer solstice (June 21)

- the autumn equinox (September 21)

- the winter solstice (December 21)[138]

The celebration of these events would help everyone to recognize four critically important annual, celestial occurrences that affect not only our entire species but every species on Earth as well. For many thousands of years, our ancestors *did* recognize and celebrate these events. In fact, their first astronomical observatories were built to determine exactly when they occurred.

People would no doubt have continued this practice if Christian clerics had not become threatened by it and forbidden it. They accomplished that in part by gradually replacing the winter solstice celebration with the Christian holiday, Christmas—and the spring equinox celebration with another Christian holiday, Easter. Fortunately, religious clerics in most societies no longer have the power to mandate which holidays can and cannot be observed.

International recognition and celebration of solstices and equinoxes would help to establish a degree of international solidarity that has never existed before. Four times each year, people everywhere on Earth would have the opportunity to celebrate something in common.

---

138 These dates would apply everywhere on Earth, except that in the southern hemisphere, they would be celebrating opposite seasons.

24: Reprioritize Loyalties

The power of being human is to care.

—Alexander Jicol

Since our ascendance into civilization, religious and cultural indoctrination has encouraged us to adopt severe anthropocentric attitudes and beliefs. Maintaining concern for ourselves and our species is natural. But the level of anthropocentrism that currently prevails encourages irresponsible behavior that leads to irreparable damage to Earth's biota and the environment. Consequently, the survival of civilization depends upon transcending, or at least moderating our anthropocentric attitudes and beliefs. Towards that end we need to reprioritize our loyalties in the following order:

- Earth

- our species

- our societies

- ourselves

These priorities are based on the premises that we cannot survive as individuals independent of societies; that societies cannot survive independent of each other; and that societies collectively cannot survive without a healthy planet on which to live. In other words, in order to survive, we need to *reverse* our priorities.

In order to demonstrate a commitment to sustainability it would help if all nations began to fly an internationally recognized Earth flag *above* their own national flags. With this simple act, we would have a constant reminder that we must learn to coexist: individuals within societies, societies within the greater community of our species, and our species within the greater community of Earth's biota.

25: Reduce Our Population

Instead of controlling the environment for the benefit of the population, maybe we should control the population to ensure the survival of our environment.

—Sir David Attenborough

According to UN predictions, there will be nine billion people on Earth by 2050 and 10.1 billion by 2100.[139] There are many problems intrinsic to artificial development that need to be addressed—but none more pressing than overpopulation. By itself, overpopulation represents the single-greatest risk to civilization. It also exacerbates other chronic problems, such as pollution, resource depletion, environmental degradation, etc. And yet, astoundingly, social leaders are unwilling to address this issue.

The reasons for their reticence are complex. But they all stem from the fact that, until recently, most societies have benefited from rampant population growth. This condition prevails, because modern nations are structured around competitive, rather than cooperative, development. Consequently, attempting to initiate population reduction—or even to curb population growth—will be met with resistance by nearly everyone. This resistance will manifest itself primarily from three conservative positions:

---

139 http://news.sciencemag.org/scienceinsider/2011/05/10-billion-plus-why-world-population.html

- state security,

- perpetuation of religions, and

- individuals' "natural" right to procreate.

OBSTACLES TO POPULATION REDUCTION

PROVIDING STATE SECURITY

Because of its violent and destructive nature, war will never be regarded as a positive aspect of civilization, but war has driven artificial development—through technological advancement—faster and further than any other single motive. Its impact on civilization has been enormous.

It is not known exactly where, when, or why the first war was fought. But it is a pretty safe bet that it was fought somewhere in the Middle East around ten thousand years ago, and that it was fought over the possession of arable land. Since then, because nations rely on competitive development, they have found it necessary to fight wars continuously to gain or maintain land and/or resources.

We are now fighting wars with far more sophisticated weapons than we did in the past, but we are fighting them for exactly the same reasons. As long as societies continue to embrace competitive development as part of their survival strategies, they will be fighting wars, and as long as they are fighting wars, they will be encouraging unrestrained population growth.

MAINTAINING ARMED FORCES

Because competitive societies fight wars, they need continuous supplies of young men to serve as soldiers and women to produce them. This is primarily why nations encourage population growth. Governments accomplish this goal by promoting national centrism and offering tax incentives to couples who produce more children. Exactly when this practice first began is not known. Augustus Caesar was encouraging population growth through tax incentives in the first century CE (Lefkowitz and Fant 1992, 121), but the practice almost certainly predates our awareness of it.

In any event, it has been such an effective strategy, that it is still used today. In the United States, for example, our tax system is structured around the number of "dependents" (future soldiers) we have. The more we produce, the greater our tax incentives are.

There is another aspect to the establishment of armed forces that needs to be addressed, because it contributes profoundly to social inequity. Typically, soldiers are recruited from financially impoverished segments of societies. Young men from poor backgrounds who are not well educated and have few opportunities for social advancement are generally easier to recruit and indoctrinate. In fact, young men from such backgrounds frequently join armies to improve their living conditions! This is why upper classes in highly competitive societies (such as the United States) strive to maintain conditions that ensure significant portions of their populations remain poor, uneducated, and reproductively prolific.

Utilizing competitive survival strategies forces artificial societies to grow perpetually larger and stronger so they can compete with and defend themselves from other competitive societies that are doing the same. Civilization has advanced almost to the point where this is no longer the case, but the inertia of past experiences encourages societies to continue to regard population growth as positive—even though, for most of them, overpopulation now threatens their future prospects more than invasion does.

SUPERIOR WEAPONRY

Another way nations have attempted to establish and maintain state security is through the development and accumulation of superior weaponry. This strategy began soon after the adoption of agriculture. Prior to 10,000 BCE, weapons with functions intended specifically to inflict bodily harm on other humans did not exist. By 8000 BCE, however, such weapons were being produced en masse for that purpose. Since then, a significant portion of our creativity has been devoted to producing ever more lethal weapons.

After the deployment of the first truly formidable weapons (such as catapults and ballistae) around 4000 BCE, predictions were made that the consequences of fighting with such horrific weapons would eventually eliminate wars. Unfortunately, that has not been the case. We now have weapons at our disposal that are too powerful to practically use, and yet wars continue to be fought.

Superior weaponry may provide nations with competitive advantages during wars, but wars are still fought by soldiers, so even nations with imposing arsenals still have to maintain large populations from which soldiers can be recruited.

ESTABLISH AN INTERNATIONAL GUARD

The most effective way to ensure state security today is through the establishment of comprehensive international allegiances. This has already, almost been accomplished with the formation of the United Nations (UN).

If the UN or some other international organization were empowered to defend national borders by responding instantly to international aggression, it is unlikely that any individual nation would ever dare to invade another one. The potential benefits of having some form of *International Guard* are enormous. Nations would no longer need to develop, or maintain, weapons of mass destruction, and more importantly, they would not have to build up, or maintain, large populations to defend themselves. If all nations felt secure from invasion, they could restore their populations to environmentally sustainable levels.

PERPETUATION OF RELIGIONS

Religions are also responsible for a great deal of population growth. Their support comes solely from adherents, so they are always striving to increase their memberships.

Unfortunately, the most expedient way for religions to increase memberships is to encourage existing members to have more children. They accomplish that goal by discouraging—or forbidding—their members from practicing birth control. Children of members are easily "brought into the fold," because they are naive, trusting, and easily indoctrinated.

It is unlikely that religions could survive today if they didn't have access to young children to indoctrinate. Their dogmas are simply too implausible to elicit much support from objective adults. Consequently, in the interest of their own self-preservation, most religions will adamantly resist population reduction—at least among their own members. Unfortunately, there is no way to break this destructive cycle other than to stop supporting religions that encourage population growth.

"RIGHT" TO PROCREATE

Many people believe it is their right, or even God's intention, to allow conceptions to occur naturally. That would be a reasonable argument if we lived in a natural state of existence, but we do not. We live in an artificial state of existence.

In natural states of existence, natural selection would prevail. Conceptions would occur almost every time a female came into estrus, but many women and/or their babies would also die due to pregnancy complications. Those who argue that it is their right to procreate naturally would then logically also have to accept the consequences of dying naturally.

In modern societies, we all benefit from artificial technologies that save or prolong our lives, but those benefits have costs and responsibilities, one of which is managing our population responsibly.

POPULATION REDUCTION

We have been incredibly irresponsible in managing our population. And as difficult as it is to manage, it will be even more difficult to reduce. Nevertheless, that is exactly what we have to do now, and the most humane and equitable way to accomplish that is by contriving birthrates.

Remarkably, we have no idea how many people Earth can support at the present time, but we do know that our current population of 6.7 billion is much too high. With objective research in the future, we will be able to determine more accurately what our population levels should be. In the meantime, it would be prudent to begin by reducing our population by 50 percent over the next fifty to sixty years. This is roughly equivalent to the population increase that occurred over the previous fifty to sixty years.

Accurately determining population-reduction statistics worldwide with all of the variables is almost impossible, because life spans vary in each country. Consequently, the projected statistics given in figure 6 are based on the following assumptions:

- the world population was 6.7 billion in 2010;

- the age of individuals is equally dispersed between zero and eighty throughout the population;

- each couple produces an average of one child;

- they produce that child when they are between twenty and forty years of age, and

- the average human life span is seventy years

If these assumptions are reasonably accurate and the following conditions are met, then the world population could be reduced at the following rate:

Ages	2010	2010–2030	2030–2050	2050–2070
60–80	1.675	1.675	1.675	1.675
40–60	1.675	1.675	1.675	.8375
20–40	1.675	1.675	.8375	.41875
0–20	1.675	.8375	.41875	.209375
Total	6.7	5.8625	4.60625	3.140625

Figure 5: Population reduction over the next 60 years

If each couple produces (on average) one child for the next sixty years, the world population will drop to 3,140,625,000 by 2070. This decrease seems like a lot, but it is actually less than the increase that occurred over the previous sixty years. For comparative purposes, if each couple averages two children, the population will remain the same, and obviously, if each couple averages more than two children, the population will continue to increase. Once our population is reduced to a sustainable level, a procreation ratio of 1:1 (two children per couple) will maintain it.

This may seem like an impossible goal to achieve, but if the public was made aware of the risks associated with overpopulation, freed from pressures imposed upon them by societies and religions to have large families, and provided with safe contraceptives, many couples would voluntarily choose to have fewer children.

For those who do not, government intervention may be necessary. Most couples regard family planning, or the lack of it, as personal matters, so they will naturally resist being told how many children they can have. But governments and religions have manipulating birth rates for thousands of years. So far, those manipulations have been used to encourage population growth, but there is no reason why they can't be used to discourage it.

Governments can accomplish that simply by offering increasingly favorable tax incentives to couples who have fewer than two children and increasingly severe disincentives to couples who have more than one child.

Obviously, this approach would have to be implemented sensibly. For example, it couldn't be applied retroactively to couples who already have more than one child or to couples who experience multiple births per pregnancy. Additionally, it would present administrative challenges when couples split up and form new partnerships, etc., but it would be an equitable way to reduce population levels. This approach is fair, because couples who produce more children place greater burdens on their society to educate and otherwise care for them.

Population reduction, especially on the scale that is suggested here, would have profound effects on societies—most of which would be both positive and predictable. But other effects, unavoidably, would not be.

We would be moving from a growth-based economy to one that was predominately based on recycling, reclamation, and restoration. Once an acceptable population level was reached, it would presumably shift into a maintenance-based economy.

Since we adopted agriculture, our competitive survival strategies have been responsible for an immense amount of damage to the environment. Some of the damage is irreversible, but environments can heal, if we protect them from further abuse. Reducing our population is a necessary step in that process.

26: Sustainability

The world we have created is a product of our thinking; it cannot be changed without changing our thinking.

—Albert Einstein

Humans have evolved in spatially separate and diverse climates and terrains over many thousands of years. This accounts for our different physical appearances and unique cultural traits. Despite these outward differences, we are still a single species. Our kinship with each other becomes evident when we look past our regional physical differences and learned cultural traits and examine our inherent traits. All humans, for example, can generally discern with a single glance the emotional state of a child,[140] regardless of where they are from. We can do this, because we are still so closely related that we "speak" the same inherent language. Additionally, regardless of where we are from, we all share the same fears, dreams, and aspirations. We all seek: peace, health, happiness, prosperity, companionship, a secure place to live, a partner to share our lives with, the right to procreate, diversity, clean air, freedom, etc. And contrary to what our political and religious leaders claim, we all recognize and adore justice, just as we all recognize and abhor injustice.

---

140 Children were chosen for this analogy because they are less adept at hiding their emotions.

The ultimate success or failure of civilization is dependent upon our realization that we are all on the same side.

There is one other critically important trait that we all share and generally fail to recognize. We have been indoctrinated to believe that our greatest adversaries are different cultures with different religious or political ideologies. But, that is not true. Our greatest adversary is, always has been, and always will be ignorance.

Visit savingcivilization.net for information about the author and links to pertinent sites regarding problems associated with civilization as well as solutions.

Appendix

GLACIALS AND INTERGLACIALS

Glacials are periods of time when Earth's mean temperature falls below 57° F (14° C). During glacials, the ratio of Earth's water to snow and ice decreases. In other words, more snow and ice accumulates in the winters than melts in the summers. Conversely, interglacials are periods of time when the ratio of Earth's water to snow/ice increases. This occurs when Earth's mean temperature rises above 57° F (14° C). In other words, more snow and or ice melts in the summers than accumulates in the winters. Conditions that affect Earth's warming and cooling cycles can be placed into two major categories: solar radiation and atmospheric insulation.

SOLAR RADIATION

Paleoclimatologists have observed that major climatic cycles last a little more than one hundred thousand years. Within these cycles, glacials last between sixty thousand and ninety thousand years, and interglacials last between ten thousand and forty thousand years (Pielou 1992, 8). Not coincidentally, these climatic cycles correspond to three astronomical events known collectively as the Milankovitch Cycles,[141] named for the Serbian mathematician who recognized and calculated them. The three cycles are identified as: eccentricity, axial tilt, and precession.

---

141 http://www.homepage.montana.edu/~geol445/hyperglac/time1/milankov.htm

ECCENTRICITY

Earth's orbit around the sun is influenced primarily by the sun's gravity. However, the gravitational forces of Jupiter and Saturn, depending upon their orbits, may elongate Earth's orbit into an ellipse. This cycle takes about one hundred thousand years to complete (fig. 7).

Logically, the closer Earth is to the sun, the more solar radiation it will receive, and the warmer it will be. Currently, the difference between perihelion (closest distance) and aphelion (farthest distance) is about 3.2 million miles, which is equivalent to about a 6.8 percent difference in solar radiation.[142] However, when Earth's orbit is at its most elliptical, the difference between the amount of solar radiation at perihelion and aphelion will be about 24 percent. Naturally, the difference in solar radiation received by Earth as a result of its eccentric orbits has profound effects on Earth's climate.

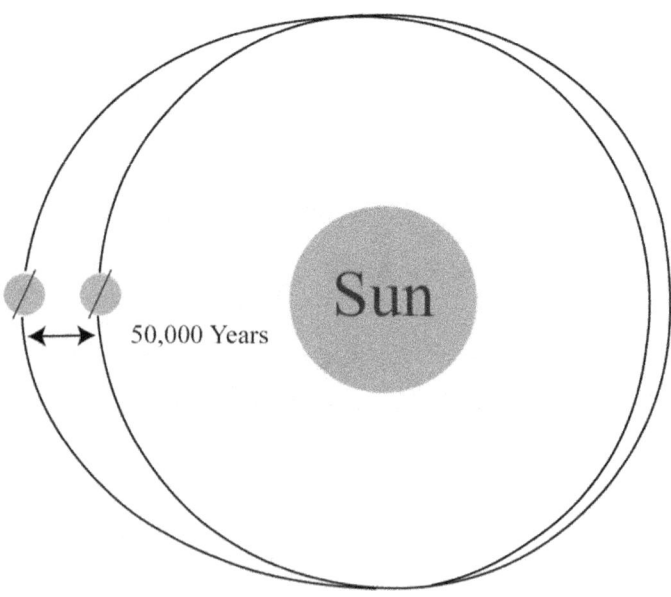

Figure 6: Eccentricity (100,000-year cycles)

AXIAL TILT

Earth spins on an axis, making a complete rotation every twenty-four hours and a complete revolution around the sun every 365 days, but it does so on a tilted axis (which is why we have seasons). From March 21 until September 21, it is warmer in the Northern Hemisphere, because Earth's axial tilt is exposing it to the sun's direct radiation. Conversely, from September 21 to March 21, it is warmer in the Southern Hemisphere, because Earth's axial tilt is exposing it to the sun's direct radiation.

However, Earth's axial tilt is not constant (fig. 8); it varies between 22.1° and 24.5° every 20,500 years in a forty-one-thousand-year cycle.[143] A 22.1° tilt correlates to milder seasons, and a 24.5° tilt correlates to more severe seasons. The dynamics of these effects are complicated and not very well understood. However, it is generally believed that Earth's climate will cool when Earth experiences milder seasons, because cooler summers do not melt off as much of the accumulated snow and ice—even though Earth receives the same total amount of solar radiation. This occurs, because solar radiation is reflected off the snow and ice back into space instead of being absorbed by Earth.

Currently, Earth's axial tilt is 23.44° and decreasing—meaning the effects of Earth's eccentricity should result in some global cooling.

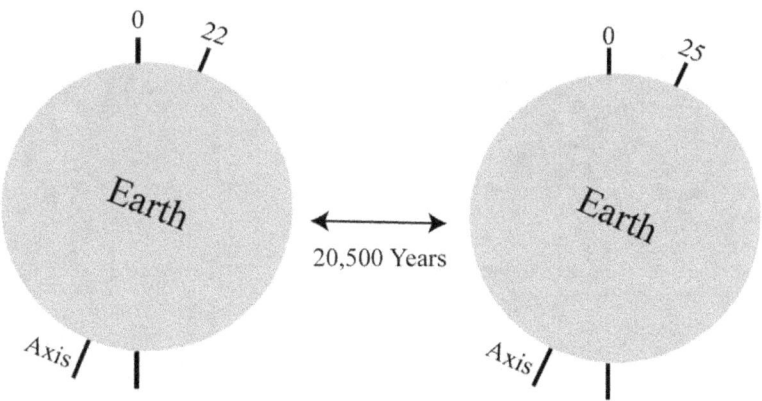

Figure 7: Axial tilt of Earth (41,000-year cycles)

143 http://www.absoluteastronomy.com/topics/Axial_tilt

PRECESSION

Besides changing by degrees, Earth's axis also revolves around its geographical center every twenty-two thousand years (fig. 9). This means that eleven thousand years from now, the weather we experience in July will occur in January, and the weather we experience in March will occur in September. Precession affects when seasons occur, but by itself, it would have no effect on climate changes. However, when viewed in conjunction with Earth's eccentric orbit, its effects are significant.

Currently, in the Northern Hemisphere, our winters occur during perihelion (when Earth is closest to the sun), which makes our winters less severe. And our summers occur during aphelion (when Earth is farthest from the sun), which makes our summers more moderate. However, in eleven thousand years, because of precession, these conditions will reverse, making our winters colder and summers warmer. What net effect this will have on Earth's climate is unknown, but it may be profound.

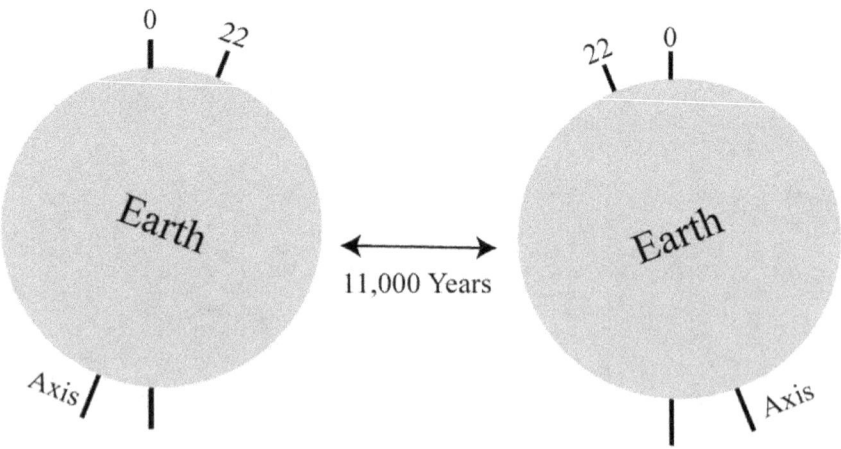

Figure 8: Precession (22,000-year cycles)

The dynamics of how the Milankovitch Cycles affect climate change are not completely understood. Nevertheless, most paleoclimatologists feel very comfortable assigning a definite correlation between them and Earth's primary cooling and warming trends.

STADES AND INTERSTADES

Existing within glacials and interglacials are cool periods called stades and warm periods called interstades. The reasons for these minor cooling and warming periods also are not well understood, but changing ocean currents, volcanic eruptions, variations in sunspot activity, and varying amounts of greenhouse gases are thought to be responsible for most of them.

SUNSPOT ACTIVITY

Sunspot activity is frequently cited as a major contributor to climate change on Earth. Sunspots are seen as dark areas on the sun's surface. People have been aware of them for thousands of years; however, sunspots could not be properly studied until the telescope was invented in the early 1600s. Since then, their occurrence, duration, and intensity have been carefully monitored and recorded.

Sunspots generally occur on alternate sides of the sun's equator in twenty-two-year cycles (eleven years on each side).[144] Sunspots are actually cooler than the rest of the sun's surface, but they are surrounded by **plages** that are much hotter. Consequently, there is a net increase in solar radiation and magnetism during increased sunspot activity.

Scientists have long noted that there was a possible correlation between stades (cooling periods) and low sunspot activity. For example, the climatic cooling period known as the Maunder Minimum,[145] or "Little Ice Age,"

144 http://www.exploratorium.edu/sunspots/research4.html
145 http://www.exploratorium.edu/sunspots/research4.html

which occurred between 1645 and 1715, corresponded to an unusually low period of sunspot activity. The simultaneous occurrence of these two events, although provocative, was not sufficient, however, to establish a definite correlation between them. With barely four hundred years of recorded sunspot activity, there simply was not enough data to substantiate a connection.

However, scientists have recently discovered—from ice core studies in Greenland—that there is a definite correlation between sunspot activity and the presence of beryllium-10 atoms on Earth, enabling them to extrapolate sunspot activity from before 1600 CE. Their findings also reflect abnormally low sunspot activity during the Spoerer Minimum (1420–1530 CE), the Wolf Minimum (1280–1340 CE), and the Oort Minimum (1010–1050 CE).[146]

Beginning in 1997, sunspot activity began to increase. By around 2002, it peaked, and in 2008, it completed its cycle. If sunspots are having a marked effect on global warming, then, barring other mitigating climate-altering conditions, the present warming trend should cease or at least diminish in the near future.

One other consideration regarding this correlation is that there was also abnormally high sunspot activity during the 1930s,[147] which was the warmest period of time on Earth since the Altithermal. Earth's current temperatures may have recently exceeded the 1930s temperatures, but it is pertinent that both of these events occurred during periods of increased sunspot activity.

---

146 http://www.exploratorium.edu/sunspots/research4.html
147 http://personal.eunet.fi/pp/tilmari/tilmari5.htm

Glossary

Unless otherwise noted, word definitions are taken from *Merriam-Webster: Webster's Third New International Dictionary, Unabridged.* (Merriam-Webster, 2002. http://unabridged.merriam-webster.com.)

agriculture - a: the science or art of cultivating the soil, harvesting crops, and raising livestock - b: the science or art of the production of plants and animals useful to man and in varying degrees the preparation of these products for man's use and their disposal (as by marketing)

allegiance - 2: devotion or loyalty especially to a person, group, or cause entitled to obedience or service and respect

antinomianism - the theological doctrine that by faith and God's gift of grace through the gospel, a Christian is freed not only from the Old Testament law of Moses and all forms of legalism but also from all law, including the generally accepted standards of morality prevailing in any given culture

apologist - 1: one who makes an apology or defense: one who speaks or writes in defense of a faith, a cause, or an institution; especially: one who makes a systematic defense of Christianity - 2 usually capitalized: one of a number of 2d century church fathers who wrote treatises in defense of the Christian faith

artificial - 1: contrived through human art or effort and not by natural causes detached from human agency: relating to human direction or effect in contrast to nature - a: formed or established by man's efforts, not by nature - b: produced or effected by man's skill to imitate nature

caliph - 1: a successor of Muhammad as temporal and spiritual head of the community and religious faith of Islam - used primarily in historical reference following Turkey's abolition of the caliphate on March 23, 1924

canola - a made-up word derived from "Canada" and "oil" [Canola is a genetically engineered plant developed in Canada from the rapeseed plant (http://www.ithyroid.com/canola_oil.htm).]

capitalism - an economic system characterized by private or corporation ownership of capital goods, by investments that are determined by private decision rather than by state control, and by prices, production, and the distribution of goods that are determined mainly in a free market

conservative - 2a : of or relating to a political party, point of view, or philosophy that advocates preservation of the established order and views proposals for change critically and usually with distrust

deception - the conveyance of disinformation intended to persuade through deceit (Author)

dogma - 1a: something held as an established opinion; especially - one or more definite and authoritative tenets b: a code or systematized formula-tion of such tenets c: a point of view or alleged authoritative tenet put forth as dogma without adequate grounds - an arrogant or vehement expression of opinion

education - the conveyance of accurate information intended to foster greater awareness (Author)

egalitarian - 1: a belief in human equality - a: a belief that all men are equal in intrinsic worth and are entitled to equal access to the rights and privileges of their society; specifically : a social philosophy advocating the leveling of social, political, and economic inequalities

equity - 1a: a free and reasonable conformity to accepted standards of natural right, law, and justice without prejudice, favoritism, or fraud and without rigor entailing undue hardship - justice according to natural law or right – fairness – impartiality

facsimile - 1: an exact and detailed copy of

faith - 2a (1): firm or unquestioning belief in something for which there is no proof - (2): uncritical grounds for belief - used chiefly in the phrase on faith

indoctrination - the conveyance of dogma intended to persuade through faith (Author)

octane - 3: motor fuel as rated by octane number (the higher the number the less likely being the fuel to detonate)

plage - 2: a bright region on the sun caused by the light emitted by clouds of calcium or hydrogen and often associated with a sunspot

Posilac - trade name of the genetically engineered variant of the natural growth hormone rBGH below (Author)

rBGH (recombinant bovine growth hormone) - a genetically engineered variant of the natural growth hormone produced by cows [formerly manufactured by Monsanto, it is sold to dairy farmers under the trade name "Posilac"]. Injection of this hormone forces cows to boost milk production by about 10 percent, while increasing the incidence of mastitis, lameness, and reproductive complications (http://www.organicconsumers.org/rbgh-link.cfm).

Roundup Ready - a term coined by Monsanto indicating a crop's resistance to "Roundup" and other glyphosate-based herbicides (Author)

socialism - 1: any of various theories or social and political movements advocating or aiming at collective or governmental ownership and administration of the means of production and control of the distribution of goods - 2a: a system or condition of society or group living in which there is no private property - b: a system or condition of society in which the means of production are owned and controlled by the state

thermohaline - circulation of ocean water caused by changes in density. This can occur as the ocean is warmed or cooled at the surface by radiation and contact with the atmosphere, or by the addition of fresh water (rain, snow, and river runoff) or salt (from formation of sea ice

(http://www.esr.org/outreach/glossary/sea_ice.html)

tularemia - an infectious zoonotic disease especially of wild rabbits, rodents, humans, and some domestic animals that is caused by a bacterium (Francisella tularensis), is transmitted especially by the bites of insects or ticks or by handling infected animals, and in humans is marked by variable symptoms - called also rabbit fever

vector - 2 a: an organism (as an insect) that transmits a pathogen

vegan - a strict vegetarian who consumes no animal or dairy products

Zoroastrianism - a Persian religion founded in the sixth century BC by the prophet Zoroaster, promulgated in the Avesta, and characterized by worship of a supreme god Ahura Mazda who requires good deeds for help in his cosmic struggle against the evil spirit Ahriman

Bibliography

Ali, Maulana Muhammad. 2002. *The Holy Qur'an with English Translation and Commentary*. Dublin, OH: Ahmadiyya Anjuman Isha'at Islam Lahore, Inc.

Barker, Kenneth L., et al., eds. 2002. *Zondervan NIV Study Bible (Fully Revised)*. Grand Rapids, MI: Zondervan.

Barry, John M. 2005. *The Great Influenza: The Story of the Deadliest Pandemic in History*. New York, NY: Penguin Group.

Brown, Raymond E. 1997. *An Introduction to the New Testament*. New York, NY: Doubleday, Inc.

Bryson, Bill. 2003. *A Short History of Nearly Everything*. New York, NY: Broadway Books.

Diamond, Jared. 1997. *Guns, Germs, and Steel: The Fates of Human Nations*. New York and London: W. W. Norton & Company.

———. 1991. *The Rise and Fall of the Third Chimpanzee: How Our Animal Heritage Affects the Way We Live*. London: Radius.

Cummins, John. 1992. *The Voyage of Christopher Columbus: Columbus' Own Journal of Discovery Newly Restored and Translated*. New York: St. Martins Press.

Gardner, Joseph L., et al., eds. 1981. *Reader's Digest Atlas of the Bible: An Illustrated Guide to the Holy Land*. Pleasantville, NY: Reader's Digest Association.

Giblin, James Cross. 1995. *When Plague Strikes: The Black Death, Smallpox, AIDS*. New York, NY: HarperCollins Publishers.

Johnson, E.A.J. 1973. *The Foundations of American Economic Freedom: Government and Enterprise in the Age of Washington*. New York, NY: University of Minnesota Press.

Kitty, Alexandra, and Robert Greenwald. 2005. *Outfoxed: Rupert Murdoch's War on Journalism*. New York, NY: The Propaganda Company, Ltd..

Lefkowitz, Mary, and Maureen B. Fant. 1992. *Women's Life in Greece and Rome: A Source Book in Translation*. Baltimore, MD: Johns Hopkins University Press.

Loewen, James W. 1995. *Lies My Teacher Told Me*. New York, NY: The New Press.

Merriam-Webster: Webster's Third New International Dictionary, Unabridged (MW). Merriam-Webster, 2002. http://unabridged.merriam-webster. com.

Nader, Ralph. 2004. *The Good Fight*. New York, NY: HarperCollins Books.

Pielou, E. C. 1992. *After the Ice Age: The Return of Life to Glaciated North America*. Chicago and London: University of Chicago Press.

Scherman, Rabbi Nosson, et al., eds. 2005. *Tanakh (Stone Edition), The Torah/Prophets/Writings: The Twenty-Four Books of the Bible Newly Translated and Annotated*. Brooklyn, NY: Mesorah Publications, Ltd.

Tabor, James D. 2006. *The Jesus Dynasty: The Hidden History of Jesus, His Royal Family, and the Birth of Christianity*. New York, NY: Simon & Schuster.

Woodward, Bob. 2004. *Plan of Attack*. New York, NY: Simon & Schuster.

www.ingramcontent.com/pod-product-compliance
Lightning Source LLC
Chambersburg PA
CBHW072356290526
45794CB00001B/83